Acknowledgments

Special thanks to Jennifer Murray, Charlene Emmett, and David Ling for their assistance in research, data gathering, and coordination. It was much appreciated.

Special thanks to my very dear friend Kirsten Tisdale for her great editorial contribution and for her valuable friendship.

Special thanks to Diane Doucet, Kim Spearns, Fred Guptill, and Jeff Morris for their wonderful feedback and editorial comments.

Special thanks to Patti Ellis Hedden for helping me put it all together.

Special thanks to my husband Miles and our three wonderful children Kaitlyn, Kara, and Andrew for their love and encouragement and support. All those "You can do it Mom!" comments were really appreciated.

Special thanks to my mom and dad, Olga and Leonard Dooley, for always being there and for instilling in me the confidence to know that I can do anything I set my mind to. It's amazing what can be done when you "know you can."

Disclaimer

The purchase of computer software or hardware is an important and costly business decision. While the author and publisher of this book have made reasonable efforts to ensure the accuracy and timeliness of the information contained herein, the author and publisher assume no liability with respect to loss or damage caused or alleged to be caused by reliance on any information contained herein and disclaim any and all warranties, expressed or implied, as to the accuracy or reliability of said information.

This book is not intended to replace the manufacturer's product documentation or personnel in determining the specifications and capabilities of the products mentioned in this book. The manufacturer's product documentation should always be consulted, as the specifications and capabilities of computer hardware and software products are sub-

Table of Contents

Chapter 9: Winning Awards/Cool Sites and More 103

Chapter 10: Maximizing Promotion with Meta-Indexes 114

Chapter 11: Productive Online Advertising 120

Chapter 13: Keep 'Em Coming Back 155

Chapter 14: Maximizing Media Relations 174

Chapter 15: Online Publications 189

Introduction

"We are crossing a technology threshold that will forever change the way we learn, work, socialize, and shop. It will affect all of us, and businesses of every type, in ways far more pervasive than most people realize."

— Bill Gates
Comdex 1994

Over the last few years there has been a veritable tidal wave of companies building web sites. This phenomenal boom in web site creation and online traffic has intensified the battle for the consumer's time and attention.

Building a web site, however, is just the first step. The logical follow-up to web site development involves a comprehensive online marketing strategy that will capture market share. The need for information and advice on developing Internet marketing strategies is tremendous.

Driving business to your site takes knowledge, planning, time, and effort. If you are intent on maintaining a competitive advantage, then you need to build your traffic by implementing an effective Internet marketing strategy.

Whether you are an experienced marketing professional, or just dreaming of starting your own Internet business, you will benefit from the information contained in this book. *101 Ways to Promote Your Web Site* offers comprehensive, hands-on, step-by-step advice for building online traffic using hundreds of proven tips, tools, and techniques. You will find out how to:

- Make your site unique and tailored to your target market
- Make sure your site attracts new visitors and keeps them coming back
- Prepare and submit to hundreds of search engines and directories, ensuring you are listed in the top search results

- Develop an effective banner ad campaign
- Use newsgroups to communicate with your market and build your reputation
- Use links, one of the most effective Internet marketing tools
- Find and use free promotion tools available on the Internet

This book was designed for entrepreneurs, corporate marketing managers, consultants, and small business owners. With this book's wealth of information on specific marketing strategies, you will be given a proven method to turn your commercial web site into an online success.

Your "Members Only" Web Site

The Internet world changes every day. That's why there is a companion web site associated with this book. On this site you will find updates to the book and other web site promotion resources of interest. However, you have to be a member of the "101 Ways Insiders Club" to gain access to this site.

When you purchased this book, you automatically became a member (in fact, that's the only way to join), so you now have full privileges. To get into the "Members Only" section of the companion web site, go to the Maximum Press web site located at *http://www.maxpress.com* and follow the links to the "101 Ways" area. From there you will see a link to the "101 Ways Insiders Club" section. When you try to enter, you will be asked for a user ID and password. Type in the following:

- For your user ID enter: *101ways*
- For your password enter: *river*

You will then be granted full access to the "Members Only" area. Visit the site often and enjoy the updates and resources with our compliments—and thanks again for buying the book. We ask that you not share the user ID and password for this site with anyone else.

1

Essentials of Web Site Design

Site design, appearance, functionality, and features are all important aspects to consider before you think about promoting your site. If the site is designed to achieve your marketing objectives, looks good, and the layout is easy to follow, you are ready to open your doors. There are many key factors to consider that may be overlooked in the initial design stages. A great domain name should be chosen and whenever possible the company's name should be used. Appropriate titles should be located on each page to identify your company and the page content. In this chapter we cover:

- How and why meta tags should be prepared for each page of your site
- The importance of each page's title, description, and keywords
- Web site features and design guidelines
- Checking out the competition
- The use of graphics

- Top-rated sites
- Encouraging repeat visits
- Incentives for increasing hits
- Corporate identity and your web site
- Guiding the search engines to you
- Ensuring your site works with different web browsers

Building Traffic to Your Site

The phrase "if you build it, they will come" worked in the movies, but it does not work with your web site. Building a web site is just the first step. Driving traffic to your site takes knowledge, planning, time, and effort. This book's focus is on increasing traffic to your web site.

To achieve the maximum marketing potential of your site, we cover several topics that relate to your web site content and design. We recommend that the following Internet marketing tips, tools, and techniques be used in conjunction with your overall web site design.

Consider Your Web Site Objectives First

Before you plan your online strategy, and certainly before you start construction of your site, it is imperative to determine your online objectives. What do you want your web site to accomplish? Do you want to sell directly to your customers? Do you want your site to provide information on your products or services? Do you want to provide customer support and service?

Determine the objectives of your web site or online presence before you begin to build the site. The most common objectives include:

- Advertising products or services
- Selling products or services
- Providing customer service or support
- Providing useful information
- Reinforcing brand image
- Providing product information cost effectively

Know your objectives and build your site around them. This will ensure satisfaction at the end of the process.

Presenting Your Web Site Message Clearly

Visitors to your web site need to know and understand your message instantly from the very first page of your web site. Direct your visitors towards your message. Do you want them to buy? Browse? Provide feedback? Order? In traditional advertisements you need to attract the attention of your audience immediately. This is also the case with your Internet audience. However, unlike traditional advertising, you can deliver more information over the Internet than you can in a 30-second commercial or a half-page print ad.

Using Competitor Sites to Your Advantage

Keeping up with the *CyberJoneses* is very important. Visit your competitors' sites for some ideas. Also visit sites that are listed on hot sites pages. Look at the design of these sites to get a better idea of what you should include in yours. Examine the colors and backgrounds used, see how the information is organized, and look at the features provided. Some good sites to go to for ideas are:

- Cool Site of the Day - *http://cool.infi.net*

- Lycos Top 250 - *http://www.lycos.com*
- Top 5% of the Web - *http://www.pointcom.com*
- Web Crawler Top 25 - *http://www.webcrawler.com*

Realizing the Potential of Your Domain Name

Domain Name
The unique name that identifies an Internet site, *www.sitename.com*

One of the most important things from an online marketing perspective, often overlooked when developing your web presence, is your **domain name**. Your Internet domain name is your exclusive web address that you can purchase through Internic, the online organization in charge of domain name registration. Having your own domain name provides you with many benefits:

- The name itself can increase traffic to your site
- Having your own domain name builds credibility for your organization
- Your presence is mobile when you own your domain name
- Internet marketing efforts travel with the domain name

Your domain name should be easy to remember and relate to your online presence. Using your company name is usually the best choice, and should be used whenever possible.

People will generally try *"www.yourcompanyname.com"* first when searching for a commercial web site. If customers or potential customers know your company exists, they will find your web site quickly and easily if your domain name is your company name. If your company name is not well known, you may choose to use a catchy descriptive phrase or the subject of your web site as its domain name. For example, imagine that you were searching for information on buying a timeshare and one of your search engine results is a site with a **URL** named *www.howtobuytimeshare.com* with accompanying text of "Free expert advice on buying a timeshare." What are the chances that you would click

URL
Uniform Resource Locator
An address on the web

through to that site? Pretty good. Keep your domain name simple, easy to remember, and related to the subject of your site.

Having your own domain name projects a professional image for your company. One of the benefits of the Internet is that it creates a level playing field for small and medium sized companies. Having your own domain name projects the image of an established business operating online in a professional manner.

Businesses that develop an online presence without registering their own domain name generally use the domain name of the **ISP** or company that is hosting their site. Your site address would generally have the following address: *http://www.yourISP.com/yoursitename*

ISP
Internet Service Provider

This type of address is not mobile, meaning you can't take it with you should you ever want to move your web site to another host. If you own your own domain name it is yours as long as you keep your registration fees current with Internic. You then have the option of moving your site to another host without losing your web address. You can change the host of your site at any time and take your domain name with you. If you allow your ISP or any other party to take care of the domain name registration process, ensure that you are listed as the actual owner of the domain so that you don't run into problems should you decide to move your site.

It takes a great deal of time and effort to promote your site online. Getting listed in all the search engines and directories, developing links to your site, and getting listed in meta-indexes all are time consuming tasks. These listings and links all automatically link the viewer to your site address. If you don't own your address, you can't take it with you if you want to move your site to another ISP or host. If you move you would lose most, if not all, of the momentum gained by your previous online marketing activities. Having your own domain name gives you the option to move your site at any time without having a negative impact on your previous marketing efforts.

When conducting business in an international environment you need the most common top-level domain name, ending in *.com*, which is used around the world. Canadian sites can use *.ca*. However, to be globally recognized you should use the *.com* designation. As mentioned earlier, when a person knows of your company and wants to visit your web site the first inclination is to check *www.yourcompanyname.com*

Your domain name must be registered with Internic. Internic Registration Services provides domain name registration services for the top-level domains: *.com*, *.net*, *.org*, and *.edu*. Registering a domain name with Internic can either be done through your ISP or you can do it yourself through the Internic web site at *www.internic.net*. If your ISP registers your domain name you should ensure that you are named as the Administrative Contact. You can do a search at the Internic web site to determine whether or not your preferred domain name is available.

The fee for registering your domain name is $70 US for the first two years and there is a $35 US renewal fee for every year thereafter. Network Solutions' registration fee covers the cost of processing the initial registration and maintaining the domain name record. The renewal fee covers one year of maintenance for the domain name record and is assessed each year on the anniversary of the original registration.

The registration process begins once you have submitted your complete and correctly formatted Agreement. Your registration request is processed immediately and you will be notified via e-mail when processing is finished. The complete process generally takes less than 24 hours, with some requests processed in as little as 10 minutes.

The Essentials of Your Web Site Design

These are web site design tips that are relevant to all web sites:

- Your online and offline corporate image should be consistent
- Your site should be easy to read
- Your site should be easy to navigate
- Your web pages should have a consistent layout
- Your web pages should be no larger than 100k

The tone of your text and the design of your graphics will convey your intended image. Keep your online image consistent with your offline image. Be consistent with the use of logo, corporate colors, and any other marketing collateral associated with your company.

Choose your background and font colors carefully. Using backgrounds that are too busy will obscure your text and will not provide a pleasant viewing experience for your visitor. Only some colors will show up properly on certain backgrounds. A light background with dark text is easiest on the eyes.

Don't set your text size too small as this is too hard to read. Don't set it too large as this looks like you are shouting!! Also, avoid using ALL CAPS, WHICH ALSO COMES ACROSS AS SHOUTING.

Use the default colors for links whenever possible. Blue text usually indicates an unvisited link. Purple, maroon, or darker blue usually represent a followed link, and red is the color of an active link. It should not be difficult for visitors to identify your links. If you decide not to use the default colors, your links should be emphasized in a consistent manner either through font size, font style, or underlines.

Ease of navigation is very important to your site. Provide a navigation bar on every page that links to all of the major pages of your site. Make it easy to get from one page to any other. Never have dead ends where viewers scroll down a page or two of information only to find that they must scroll all the way back up to the top to move on (because you have no links at the bottom of the page). Also avoid dead links. These are links that don't go anywhere and the viewer usually receives an error message after clicking on them. Verify periodically that all your links are still active.

Your visitors should be able to get anywhere they want to go on your site in three clicks or less.

Keep the design of your site consistent. Font types, headers, footers, navigational bars, buttons, bullets, colors, etc. should be consistent throughout the site to maintain a polished professional look.

> **Home Page**
> The main web page of a web site

Your **home page** should be 50k or less, and your home page should be displayed on one or two screens. Studies have shown that visitors will rarely wait beyond 15 seconds to download a site. Test the download time of your site with a 14.4 modem to ensure that it is reasonable for all users.

Keeping Web Site Graphics in Perspective

Graphics are pleasant to look at but be discriminating when adding them to your site. Graphics that are too time-consuming to download may cause visitors to leave your site before they get a chance to see it. Remember that a lot of Internet users are still using 14.4 or 28.8 modems. Keep your graphics files under 50k. Some people turn graphics off in their browsers to save time, so you should provide all of your information in text as well as graphics. If you use any large files for graphics, audio, or video, warn your visitors by providing some text stating the size of the files.

Provide Ease of Navigation with User Friendly Site Maps

For very large sites it is a good idea to include a site map which users can access from any page in your site. Site maps, as shown in Figures 1.1 and 1.2, are usually text-based lists that name all of the site's pages and their content. Site maps make it easy for users to access the information they are looking for without causing them much frustration.

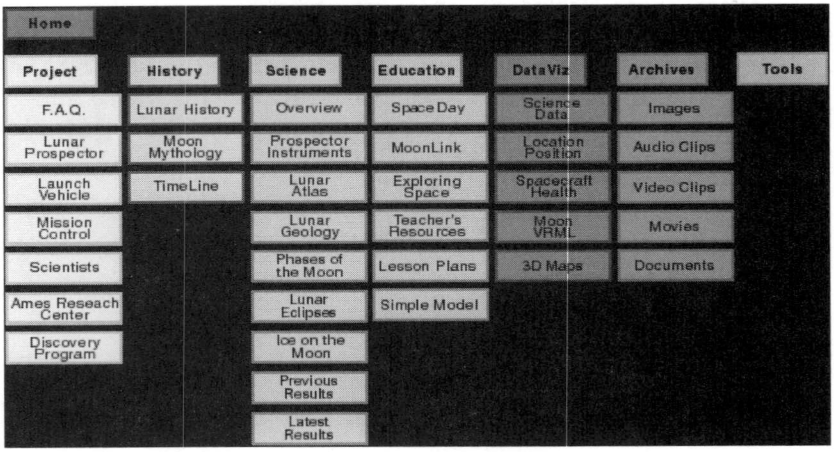

Figure 1.1. Most site maps are provided in a tree structure and provide the user with an easy way to navigate a large site.

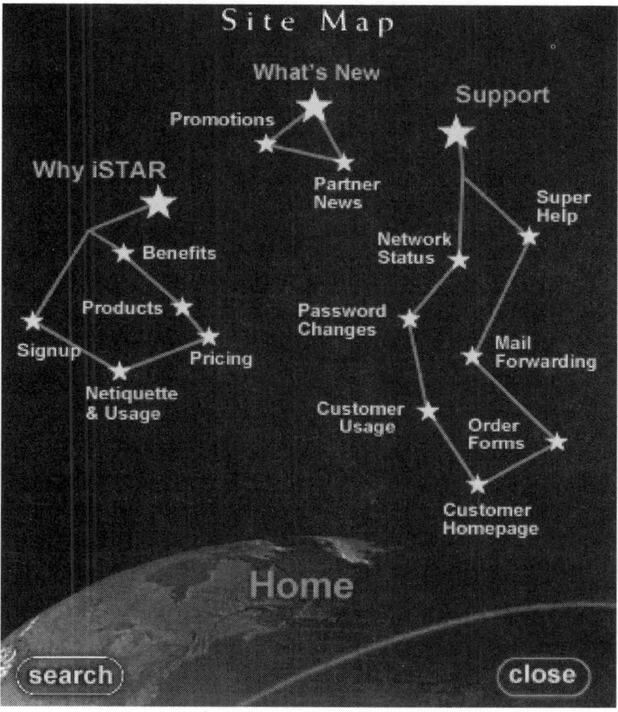

Figure 1.2. Other site maps are a little more innovative in their graphics and still provide the user easy access to every page of the site.

Identify Your Site with Page Titles

Each of the pages in your web site should be given a title. A title is a piece of information in your HTML document that is used as identification for your pages. Titles can tell readers where the information contained on a page originated. Most web browsers, such as Netscape, display a document's title in the top line of the screen. When users print a page from your web site the title usually appears at the top of the page at the left. When someone bookmarks your site, the title appears as the description in their bookmark file. These are all reasons why it is important that a page's title reflects an accurate description of the page.

Go through each and every page of your Internet site, bookmark each one, and check that your titles represent each page clearly without being lengthy. The titles should always identify your company. Examples of appropriate titles are:

- "Progeny Software - Genealogy Software Specialists"
- "Progeny Software - Free Trial Version"

And inappropriate titles are:

- "The Best Software Page on the Web"
- "The Software Home Page"

The titles of your pages should be changed periodically as this allows your site to be re-submitted and re-indexed by the search engines.

Viewing Your Site Through Browser Eyes

Browsers Software programs that let you "surf" the Internet

Check your site using different **browsers**. What the viewer sees when your site is downloaded depends on what browser they are using. Different browsers will display the same web site differently. Check your site with the most popular browsers. They are:

- Netscape Navigator 4.0
- Netscape Navigator 3.0
- Netscape Navigator 2.0
- Microsoft Internet Explorer 4.0
- Microsoft Internet Explorer 3.0
- America Online 4.0

Choosing Web Site Features to Meet Marketing Objectives

Chat Room
A site where you can chat, in real time, with others

There are many features that can be incorporated into your web site. It is important to look at each feature from both marketing and administrative views before deciding to incorporate it into your site. A **chat room** might seem like a neat feature to have at first blush, but you have to ask the questions: "What is the marketing value to our company in having this on our web site? Will it increase targeted traffic to our site? Will it encourage repeat visits from our customers and potential customers? Will it result in increased sales?

Assuming that you can justify a chat room on your site from a marketing perspective, then you must look at the feature from a financial perspective. What will this feature cost to develop? What will be the ongoing costs of operating this feature in technical resources as well as in human resources? What is our budget? Can these resources provide a better return on investment if spent elsewhere? Would we achieve our objectives more effectively if we put these financial resources into banner advertising or other online marketing activities?

Web Trak has performed a survey to examine which features are being included in web sites. The following features were found on web sites in the study with the frequency reported below:

- Feedback Mechanisms – 25%
- FAQs – 24%
- Contest Competitions – 24%
- Press Releases – 21%
- Downloadable Files – 17%
- What's New Sections – 16%
- Audio Content – 16%

- Surveys of Visitors – 14%
- Lists of Links – 14%
- Video Content – 11%
- Employment Opportunities – 5%
- Registration – 4%
- Interactive Chat Lines – 3%
- Interactive Bulletin Boards – 3%

Customer-Enticing Traffic Builders

Not only are the valuable features and statistics referenced above worth considering, the following "traffic builders" are used to attract and invite visitors to your site:

Free Offers

People love to get something for nothing. Offering something for free is a good way to get lots of traffic to your site. This is great if your objectives include generating lots of general user traffic to your site. Free offers also provide you the opportunity to be linked from the many **meta-indexes** related to freebies and giveaways. If you are giving something away you might consider tying it into a registration for your newsletter or mailing list. Some of the things commonly given away include screensavers, icons, software, and games. You should relate giveaways to your company, your products, or your services.

Meta-Indexes A collection of URLs for related Internet resources

Online Seminars

Online seminars are generally conducted through live chat sessions. Seminars allow customers and potential customers to interact in a real-time setting with industry experts and celebrities. This can be a great traffic builder.

Advice Columns

Advice columns are a great way to increase traffic and to gain the respect of your customers. Many companies answer questions that pertain to their products and industry. They also help their customers solve common problems with expert advice. For example, customers on the Tide web site can ask questions about how to get certain stains out of their clothes.

Coupons

Coupons are an effective way to increase traffic to your site. If your coupons are valuable and you change them daily or weekly, you will encourage visitors to return frequently.

Contests

Contests are very popular online, particularly when prizes are involved. To encourage repeat visits you should change the contest regularly or design it in such a way that your visitors can enter often. To get some information about the people who are visiting your site, and to help you with your marketing efforts, include a few pertinent questions on the entry form.

Surveys

Surveys are a popular feature for specific industries. Here, you should make sure the information you are gathering is of value to the industry and promise to provide a copy of the final report to all that participate.

Interactive Tours

Interactive tours take your visitors on a virtual tour of your offices, your factory, or your web site. Visitors can find out how a product is made or how your company operates. This is a great way to provide information on the quality of your materials and workmanship.

Guiding the Search Engines with Meta-Information

Search Engines
Programs that find something on the Net for you

Direct-ories
Similar to search engines in funtion-ality

A common problem faced by Internet marketers is how to get search engines to index their site appropriately and how to ensure that their site appears when people use relevant search criteria. Many of the interesting and creative sites on the Internet are impossible to find and are, therefore, not seen by a large portion of web users. The majority of Internet users employ **search engines** or **directories** to find web sites, which they do by typing in a keyword or phrase that represents what they are looking for.

Retaining a certain measure of control over how search engines deal with your web sites is a major concern. Often web sites do not take advantage of the techniques available to control search engine listings. The "Meta-HTML" tag can be used to tell search engines how to list a web site in their indexes.

The Web Developer's Virtual Library defines a Meta-HTML tag as follows:

> *"An HTML tag used in the Head area of a document to specify further information about the document, either for the local server, or for a remote browser. The Meta element is used within the Head element to embed document Meta information not defined by other HTML elements. Such information can be extracted by servers/clients for use in identifying, indexing, and cataloging specialized document Meta information. In addition, HTTP servers can read the contents of the document head to generate response headers corresponding to any elements defining a value for the attribute HTTP-EQUIV. This provides document authors with a mechanism for identifying information that should be included in the response headers of an HTTP request."*

To summarize this lengthy definition, meta information can be used in identifying, indexing, and cataloging. This means you can use these tags to guide the search engines in displaying your site as the result of a query.

Meta and Header Elements

A header without meta information will look like this:

```
<html>

<head>

<title> Game Nation - Gaming Software Specialists</title>

</head>
```

If you want your site to be displayed properly in search engines, you should create a header as follows:

```
<HTML>

<HEAD>

<TITLE>Document Title Here</TITLE>

<META NAME="keywords" CONTENT="keyword1,
keyword2, keyword3">

<META NAME="description" CONTENT="200-character
site description goes here">

<META NAME="robots" CONTENT="index, follow">

<!—Comments Tag, repeat description here?>
```

</HEAD> indicates the beginning of the header, and the ending of the header is marked by </HEAD>

indicates the title of the page. The end of the title is marked by </TITLE> which is called the closing tag.

<META NAME="keywords" CONTENT="... "> tells search engines under which keywords to index your site under. When a user types one of the words you listed here, your site should be displayed as a result. A space must be used to separate the words. Do not repeat any of the words more than 5 times (a lot of the **bots** will not recognize repeat words). And, you should list the most important words first because

BOTS
Intelligent agents (or robots) that search the Internet for content to put into search engines

some bots only read the first 200 characters. You should create a keywords tag for each page of your site listing appropriate keywords for each separate page.

<META NAME="description" CONTENT="..."> this should be added to every page of your site. It is used to provide an accurate description of the page to which it is attached. Keep the description under 200 characters, or it may be cut off when displayed by the search engines.

<META NAME="robots" CONTENT=" "> tells certain bots to follow or not follow hypertext links. The W3 Consortium white paper on spidering (spiders are defined below) offers the following definition and discussion:

> <META NAME="ROBOTS" CONTENT="ALL | NONE | NOINDEX | NOFOLLOW">
>
> default = empty = "ALL" "NONE"
> = "NOINDEX, NOFOLLOW"
>
> The filler is a comma-separated list of terms:
>
> ALL, NONE, INDEX, NOINDEX,
> FOLLOW, NOFOLLOW.

Note: This tag is meant to provide users who cannot control the robots.txt file at their sites. It provides a last chance to keep their content out of search services. It was decided not to add syntax to allow robot specific permissions within the META-tag INDEX means that robots are welcome to include this page in search services.

FOLLOW means that robots are welcome to follow links from this page to find other pages. A value of NOFOLLOW allows the page to be indexed, but no links from the page are explored (this may be useful if the page is a free entry point into pay-per-view content, for example. A value of NONE tells the robot to ignore the page."

The values of INDEX and FOLLOW should be added to every page unless there is a specific reason why you do not want your page to be indexed. This may be the case if the page is only temporary.

<!—Comments Tag, repeat description here?—!> is a tag that is read by the Excite and Magellan spiders. A spider is an artificial intelligence agent that reads all of the information on a page and develops a "page description." The comments tag can be used to trick a spider into displaying an accurate description of your pages. The description that a spider creates without this tag is often not pleasing, and usually doesn't depict what your pages are actually about.

Internet Resources for Chapter 1

Review Your Site

Web Site Garage
http://www.websitegarage.com
This is a one-stop shop for servicing your web site. Here, you can run critical performance diagnostics on your entire Web site and ensure browser compatibility by seeing your site in 18 different browsers, platforms, and screen sizes. This speed ups your site by optimizing your images and drives traffic to your web site. Provided is a comprehensive registration with up to 400 search engines, directories, and award sites. With this tool you can announce news through a Business Wire press release. You can target your industry, an Internet population, and analyze your web site traffic with a customizable tracking tool. This site will allow you to run a number of diagnostics on your site for free, including: spellcheck, browser compatibility, load time, link popularity, and HTML design.

Net Mechanic
http://www.netmechanic.com
This site will check your web site to find broken links, perform HTML validation to make sure the format is compatible with the most common browsers, optimize your images for quicker loading, and moni-

tor your server's performance for speed checking with different modem speeds. NetMechanic is a free online service.

Northern Webs
http://www.northernwebs.com
Northern Webs' Engine Tutorial is one of the most recognized leaders in exposing the nuances of the various search engines and explaining what makes them tick. See if your site can stand the test of their exclusive Meta Medic!

Marketsuite Mall
http://www.marketsuite.com
Marketsuite Mall has a group of free online tools that analyze your web pages. The suite includes seven utilities. Key Position checks to see if your position is among the top ten listed sites with nine search engines. SpaMalyzer checks your pages for items that the engines might consider spamming (inappropriate use of the net). Analyzer rates your pages, by percentage of optimum, for good placement with reference to your important keywords. Site Mapper maps your site for you. ProSubmit submits pages to major search engines. RemoteLinx determines who is linking to your site. MetaGen creates your meta tags for you. These utilities are all free when you sign up with a password.

Interactive Tools
http://www.arrowweb.com/graphics/tools.html
This site includes Interactive tools for web masters and site designers. Use these tools to submit and promote your web site or to find problems. Utilities are included, such as an encyclopedia, dictionary, complete reference, and search tools.

Meta Tags

Meta Tags & Search Engines
http://www.webdigger.com/meta_tags.htm
Need to improve your search engine standings? Here are a few ideas to get you started: meta tags as well as search engine and web site design tips.

Meta Tag Analyzer
http://www.scrubtheweb.com/abs/meta-check.html
This will check your meta tags and your HTML code to help you achieve better placement in search engine results. Let their free Meta Tag Analyzer Program check your meta tags and help analyze your HTML syntax online.

META Builder
http://vancouver-webpages.com/META/mk-metas.html
The META Builder will generate HTML meta tags suitable for inclusion in your HTML document. These tags allow better indexing by robot-driven search engines, such as Alta Vista and Infoseek—and now include some DCJite elements.

Meta Tag Generator
http://www.siteup.com/meta.html
The Meta Tag Generator will automatically generate meta tags used by search engines to index your pages. SiteUp Internet Promotions is proud to offer to the entire Internet community a free download of the Windows 95 Meta Tag Generator.

How to Use Meta Tags Tutorial
http://searchenginewatch.com/webmasters/meta.html

World of Design
http://www.globalserve.net/~iwb/search_engine/killer.html
This is a tutorial for writing meta tags for higher search engine placement and good descriptions.

References

Web Developers Virtual Library
http://www.stars.com
A comprehensive illustrated encyclopedia of web technology, the WDVL is for web masters and Internet developers. It's a well-organized gold mine of tutorials, demos, and links to great resources.

Whatis.com
http://www.whatis.com
Whatis.com is "definition" paradise. It defines any computer-related word you ever wondered about.

WWW Meta Indexes and Search Tools
http://www.fys.ruu.nl/~kruis/h3.html
This is a Library of Congress Internet Resource Page.

Argus Clearinghouse
http://www.clearinghouse.net
The premier Internet research library or meta-index to locate everything you need to find on the web.

A Dictionary of HTML Meta Tags
http://vancouver-webpages.com/META

Graphics

The Gif Wizard
http://www.gifwizard.com
You can reduce all your graphics using the Gif Wizard Site Scan Monitor, a free service from Raspberry Hill Publishing.

2

Maximizing Exposure with Search Tools

Let's assume your site is now ready to submit to search engines and directories where it must be found easily by your customers and prospective clients. You need to be listed in as many search engines as possible. Who knows which is the preferred directory or search engine of your potential client? When people conduct Internet searches they rarely go beyond the first few pages of results. You need to appear in the top 20 search results to be noticed. In this chapter we cover:

- The most popular search engines used today
- Description and keyword criteria for submitting to search engines
- Submitting to spiders, crawlers, and bots
- Techniques to position yourself high in search results
- Keeping a log on search engine and directory submissions

- Multiple search engine submission sites
- Submitting to special interest sites
- Search tool resources

Gaining Visibility on the Internet

There are a variety of search tools (search engines, directories, spiders, etc.) currently used to navigate the World Wide Web. Due to the unprecedented growth of the information available on the Internet, there has been an unqualified demand for simplifying this information. As a result, the creation of search tools has catapulted. In order to maintain a competitive edge, it is absolutely imperative that your web site be registered with as many search tools as possible.

A Georgia Tech survey found that people find web sites using the following methods:

- Search engines 87%
- Links from other sites 85%
- Printed media 63%
- Word of mouth 58%
- Newsgroups 32%
- E-mail 32%
- Television 32%
- Books and magazines 28%
- Other 28%

Search Engines and Their Nomadic Bots

The most common search tool is the search engine. Search engines use programs or intelligent agents, called bots, to actually search the Internet for pages, which they index using specific parameters as they read the content. The agent will read the information on every page of your site and then follow the links. To register with search engines you simply submit your URL on their submission form. Even if your URL is not registered with search engines, they will eventually find you since these bots are continually roaming the Internet looking for new sites to index. The bots will periodically visit your site looking for changes and updates.

Some search engines cannot follow **image map** links. If you only have these links on your home page, some search engines won't be able to read all of your pages. Make sure that your page is easy to navigate with **hyperlinks**. This will ensure that search engines will find all of your pages.

Some Internet marketers are trying various techniques to trick the search engines into positioning them higher in search results. These techniques are considered cheating by many Internet users. It is up to you whether you want to risk discovery by the search engines or **flames** from other marketers by implementing them. These tricks do not work with every search engine, and if it is discovered you are trying to dupe the search engines, some may not list you at all. They have been programmed to detect some of these techniques and you will be penalized in some way if you are discovered. A few of the search engine tricks are as follows:

- Repeating keywords over and over again hidden in your HTML. For example <!games, games, games, games, games,…>

- Repeating keywords over and over again by displaying them at the bottom of your document after a number of line breaks.

Image Map
A graphical image where a user can click on different areas of the image and be linked to different destinations

Flame
A harsh message to criticize or insult someone for something they have posted

Hyperlinks
An automatic link that connects a word, phrase, or a picture on one web page to another web page

- Repeating keywords by displaying them in your document using a very small font or by making the text color the same as the background color.

- Making frequent and regular title changes so that the bots think your site is a new site and they list you again and again.

- Changing the name of your site to have a space, exclamation mark (!) or 'A' as the first character so that you come up first in alphabetical lists.

Any time you make significant changes to your site you should resubmit your site to the search engines. Search engines normally revisit on a regular schedule. However, these search engines are growing smarter every day—some monitor how often the site is updated and adjust their "revisit" schedule accordingly.

Maximizing Findability with Directories

Unlike search engines, directories will not find your site if you do not tell them about it. Directories do not use bots or other intelligent agents to scour the Internet for new pages.

In order to be listed in a directory you need to submit or register your site information and URL address. This is best accomplished by visiting all the directories in which you want to be listed and filling out the required form. The registration forms are all quite similar and generally require information such as your URL, the name of your site, a description of your site, a list of keywords, your contact information, and other information depending on the particular directory. You must complete the form and click on the submit button to complete the registration process.

FAQ
Frequently Asked Questions

Know your search engines and directories. Each one is different, using different mechanisms to determine which sites rank highly. They also use different mechanisms to provide a description of your site and allow different lengths for a description. See Appendix C for details on popular search engines and directories. These are constantly changing, so to stay current you should follow up with a visit to the search engine and directory web sites and read their instructions and **FAQs**.

Some directories automatically include the information you have submitted while others review and approve your site for inclusion. The latter can take up to a month.

Content Tips for Spider and Crawler Discoveries

Spiders and crawlers Programs that visit Web sites and read their pages to create entries for a search engine index

Spiders and crawlers can find your site regardless of whether or not you actually submitted it. Check to see if they have already found your site before submitting your URL. When a spider adds your page to its database it uses the title found in the <TITLE> tag of your HTML code, hence using good descriptive titles is very important. Different spiders use different methods to index a site. It will index a portion of the page or it will index the entire page. Numerous keywords should be used on your home page to ensure that people who are looking for your type of company will find you. For example, Lycos uses the first 200 characters in the description, yet indexes the 100 most important words on each page. InfoSeek takes the first 250 characters of a site for its description.

For your site to be listed higher in search results, you must do a fair bit of research and adjust your submission accordingly. WebCrawler, for example, will give your site a higher ranking if the word the user is employing as the keyword of the search (vacation, graphics, boats, whatever) appears many times in the first paragraph or so of the page. Print your home page to get an idea of what may be listed for your site after you submit and your site is indexed. Check to ensure that this is an accurate portrayal of your site.

Because spiders will index pages other than your home page, you should go through this process for your entire site. Remember to have good navigational tools on every page of your site—you never know where your prospective customer is going to enter the site!

The All-Important Web Page Ranking Systems

When you do a search on the Internet, in seconds the search engine has digested what you are looking for, searches the millions of pages it knows about, and responds to your request with appropriate sites ranked in order of importance. Amazing! How do they do it?

Each of the search engines has its own method of ranking and determining which pages match your search criteria. They each have ranking criteria which generally revolves around the frequency and location of keywords on the web page.

Some search engines determine how often a keyword appears on the web page. It is assumed that if a keyword is used more frequently on a page, then that page is more relevant than other pages with a lower usage of that keyword. Some search engines look for the keyword in the title of the web page and assume that if the keyword is in the title, then that page must be more relevant than those that don't have the keyword in their title. Some search engines determine where keywords are used and assume that pages with the keyword in headings and in the first couple of paragraphs are more relevant. Some search engines use the number of links pointing to a particular page as part of their ranking criteria. Some search engines use information contained in meta tags and others don't look at the meta tags at all.

To summarize, search engines all have different ranking criteria and this is why you receive different results when you search on the same keyword with different engines. For each of the major search engines you should learn as much as you can about their ranking system and adjust your submission or your site's content accordingly. One site that is particularly useful with this information is *http://searchenginewatch.com*

Maximizing Exposure with Submission Pointers

Submitting to the search engines and directories is a very time consuming, but extremely important task. Don't rush! Take your time, do your research, know the ranking strategy employed and prepare your submission for optimal results. It's very difficult to change your entry once it has been submitted and the last thing you want is a typo. If the time available for indexing is limited, start by focusing on the most popular directories for individual submissions and use a multiple submission site for the less important ones. 95% of all Internet traffic is via the following search engines and directories:

- Infoseek
- Excite
- WebCrawler
- HotBot
- Alta Vista
- Yahoo!
- Lycos
- Northern Light

When submitting to the search engines and directories, take the time up front to develop the submission material. Organize the information in a logical order in a text file that remains open in the background when filling out the submission forms. This will enable you to copy and paste the content to the appropriate fields on the submission form. Be sure to spellcheck, check, and recheck everything before you start. Spellcheckers won't pick up misspelled "works" if that word is also in the dictionary. The information prepared for each page on the site to be indexed should include:

- URL
- Page title
- 10-word, 25-word, 50-word and 100-word descriptions for the page (different engines allow different lengths of description)
- List of keywords for each page (see the Keyword section of this chapter for tips)
- Description of the ideal audience for the site

- Contact information:
    - Company name
    - Contact name
    - E-mail address
    - Company address
    - Telephone and fax numbers

Print the submission forms for the various search engines and directories and examine them to determine that you have all the information required for submission.

When submitting forms to directories be very careful to fill in every field on the form. Some of the search engines will reject your registration automatically by deleting it if you have not filled in all the blanks.

When you have to choose categories select them very carefully. It would be a shame to have a great product, great price, and a great site but be listed in a place where your potential customer would never think about looking for you.

Read the FAQs or instructions first to ensure that you understand exactly what information they are requesting.

Proofread your submission at least twice before you hit the submit button. It isn't quick or easy to change listings if you make a mistake. Your listing may be wrong for quite a while before it gets corrected.

Learn from Competitor Sites

When preparing your information to submit to the various search engines and directories you will have to prepare a good description of your site as well as a listing of appropriate keywords. Some good market research will assist you here. Check out your competition. Search their names and see what they are using for descriptions. Next, search using some of your keywords and see what sites receive top ranking. This research will illustrate why they have received such a high ranking—and you can incorporate that strategy into your submission for that search engine or directory. Remember that if you don't appear in the first two or three pages of search results, it is unlikely the prospective visitor will access your site through the search engine.

Check the *View Document Source* to see what your competitors have for Meta Tags. Not only can you learn from the sites that catch your eye, you can also learn from your competitors' mistakes. After you have done a thorough job of this market research you will be in a good position to develop a description that is catchy and adequately describes your site.

Marketing Implications of Page Titles

Make sure every page in your site is titled properly for marketing purposes. The <TITLE> tag is the first item a search agent reads. Don't just use your company name—use a descriptive title and make sure you include some keywords. As mentioned earlier, some search engines use your page titles in their ranking equation. Pages that have keywords in the title are seen as more closely relevant than similar pages on the same subject that don't, and are thus ranked in a higher position by the search engine.

Keywords Are of Key Importance

When creating your keyword list, don't just use nouns. Think of descriptive words that may be associated with benefits of your products or services. For example, if your site offers information on weight loss, then some of your keywords may be "weight, weight loss, diet, exercise, nutrition," and so on. You can also add some keywords that describe advantages a person may receive from visiting your site such as "thin, slim, attractive, healthy, in shape, etc."

When determining what your keywords will be, always keep the customer or your target visitor in mind. Try to think like they would if they were to do a search for information on your topic. Don't just think about what people would do to find *your* site, but what they would do if they didn't know your company existed. They are looking for the types of products and services you provide. If you find this a difficult exercise, then ask around. Talk to both people that know about your business and people that don't. Ask what keywords they would use to find a site like yours.

Start by taking the company's brochures and other corporate marketing materials, as well as the site itself, and highlight any words that individuals might search for if they are looking for the products or services the company has to offer). Record these words in a text document in your word processing program.

Next, edit the list by deleting words that are either too broad (for example, "business") or are not appropriate for keyword purposes. Always use the plural when forming your keywords (adding an "s" forms the plural). If you list "game" as your keyword and someone uses "games" to do a search, then your site will not be found. However, if you use "games" and someone requests information on the word "game," then your site will be found because "game" is part of the word "games." If the plural does not include the singular in its entirety, for example "company" and "companies," you should list both the singular and the plural as part of your keyword list.

Now, reorganize the remaining keywords in order of importance. By having the most important words first, no matter how many keywords the particular directory will allow, you are ready to submit.

Now you have a good master keyword list. Different directories allow for different numbers of keywords to be submitted. Because you have organized your list with the most important words first, you simply include as many of your keywords as the directory will allow. When a directory will allow multiple submissions for the same URL, you might consider submitting as many times as it takes to include all your keywords. You won't have to change your description or other information every time, just the keywords.

If you plan to submit every page of your site, your master list provides a valuable document. For each page that you are indexing, take a photocopy of the comprehensive list and delete words that are not appropriate for that particular page. Then reprioritize the remaining keywords based on the content of the page you are indexing. This is then the keyword list for that page. Repeat this procedure for every page you will be indexing.

If you make changes to your web pages, change the title and keywords contained in the title as well. This will allow you to be re-indexed by search engines.

You may want to include your competitors' names in your keywords. This follows the premise that if someone searches for them they will find you as well. There is, however, an ongoing debate as to whether this is ethical.

Your keyword list should be included in your submissions to directories and in a keyword meta tag. However, to be listed in a higher position in search results you should include your most important keywords in other places as well, such as:

- Your page title
- Your description
- The first 200-250 characters of your page
- If frames are used, between the <noframes> tags
- In alt tags

Some search engines rank sites by how early the keyword appears on the site. The earlier a keyword is mentioned on your site, the earlier your site may be mentioned in search results. And remember the points made earlier...though you don't want to repeat a keyword hundreds of times (some search engines are on to this), you do want to repeat keywords a number of times on each page of your site.

Search Engines' Use of Alt Tags

Some search engines will include information within "alt tags" when they form the description for your site. Alt tags appear after an image tag and contain a phrase that is associated with the image. For example:

<image src="logo.gif" alt="Game Nation - Computer Games Logo">

This gives your page a better chance of being described correctly because you are again repeating the theme of your page.

Put text between the <noframes> tags. Some search engines see frames as internal links. They will read your main page and then return later to index your links. To get the search engine to index your page properly you must put some information about your page between the <noframes>...and...</no frames> tags. The information you put here will serve you best if it is descriptive and includes as many keywords as possible.

Great Descriptions Make the Difference

It is a good idea to create a number of different descriptions of varying lengths because the different search engines and directories allow different description sizes. Start off creating a description of 10 words, then 25, then 50, then 100. Make sure that you use the right length description for each search engine because you don't want it to be truncated when displayed in search results.

Your description should be compelling. When you get your site to appear in the first 20 to 30 top results of a search, the description is what differentiates your site from the rest. It is the description that will entice the prospective visitor to click and visit—or pass and go to a more exciting site.

Include a <comments> tag description that is the same as your Meta Tag description. You can repeat this a couple of times if you wish. It is used by the Excite spider, and if repeated may yield a more accurate description of your site.

Get Multiple Listings

One way to get your site listed many times is to submit many times. Due to the simple fact that each page on your site has a unique URL, you can submit each URL (each page) in the various search engines, directories, etc. Each different page of your site should be indexed so that there are a number of ways to reach your site. Every page should have different titles, different descriptions, and different keywords. This way people will find your site when searching for a number of criteria.

It is important to abide by netiquette. In some search sites the previously discussed practice of submitting multiple times is acceptable and may even be encouraged. In others it is considered abuse and is discouraged. Use your judgement on this one!

Effective Use of Multiple Submission Services

There are many multiple search engine submission services available on the net that will submit your site to varying numbers of indexes, directories, and search engines. They will register your URL, description, and keywords. Check them to see how comprehensive they are before using these services. Here are a couple of sites for you to look at:

The Postmaster
http://www.netcreations.com/postmaster
This is one of the best URL submission services on the web.

Add-Me
http://www.addme.com
This site allows you to submit your page to 34 popular sites for free, using one form.

Submit-It
http://www.submit-it.com/
Submit-It is one of the oldest and most respected submission services.

Register It
http://netannounce.register-it.com
Register It is a respected submission service.

Although these services save a lot of time, it is essential that you are registered accurately in search engines and directories. For the best results register individually in as many of the top search engines as you can before you resort to multiple submission sites. There aren't that many search engines or directories that have long submit forms, so submit manually to ensure the best results. Especially if you taken the time to do the work described above, submit to the major engines yourself. This way you can take full advantage of the legwork you have done targetting the differences between the engines.

To summarize, each search engine is different. Know the unique qualities of each before you submit and be sure to check out Appendix C of this book where details are provided on many of the popular search engines and directories.

Keep a Record

Keep a record of the directories and search engines to which you have submitted. The information recorded should include the following:

1. Date of the submission
2. URL of the page submitted
3. Name of the search engine or directory
4. Description used
5. Keywords used
6. Password used
7. Notes section for any other relevant information
8. Date listed

Internet Resources for Chapter 2

Web Position Analyzer
http://www.webposition.com
Software that tells you where your site is positioned in search results of the 10 most popular search engines. Builds traffic by track-

ing your search engine positions and helping you improve your rankings.

Position-It
http://www.position-it.com
How to use Internet search engines and directories to "sky rocket" your web site traffic using Search Engine Secrets for Top Positioning.

Search Engine Watch
http://www.searchenginewatch.com
Search Engine Watch is a web site devoted to how search engines work, search engine news, search engine information, tips on using search engines, and more about search engines. More information than you can stand! Be sure to sign up for the Search Engine Report mailing list.

Internet InfoScavenger
http://www.infoscavenger.com/engine.htm
Internet InfoScavenger is a monthly newsletter publication devoted to helping busy professionals market their products and services on the web. Invaluable help, techniques, and tips for top search engine placement.

Position Agent
http://www.positionagent.com
This is a great utility that will automatically check your ranking on 10 top search engines for free.

WebReference.com
http://www.webreference.com/content/search
Search engines and examples, tips, and hints for getting the most out of your search engine, for people who work on the web.

Net Promote
http://www.cyberpromotion.com
Net Promote has Promotion 101, a Web Site Marketing and Promotion Info Center, where you can find all kinds of free articles, resources, tools, and links to help you promote your site. They also offer web site registration, web site consultation, press release distribution, site launch, banner advertising, consulting, and more.

Submission Tools

The Spider

http://www.k-on-line.com/~wwtravel/welcome.htm

A great site submission tool. The Web Promotion Spider promotes your web page on the Internet in search engines and directories. Additionally, the site provides you with 450 submission sites with which you can register individually yourself. The site also provides tools and information for your submission.

SubmitPlus

http://submitplus.bc.ca/jayde

SubmitPlus (shown in Figure 2.1) helps you promote your web site with two very effective web site announcement programs. The first

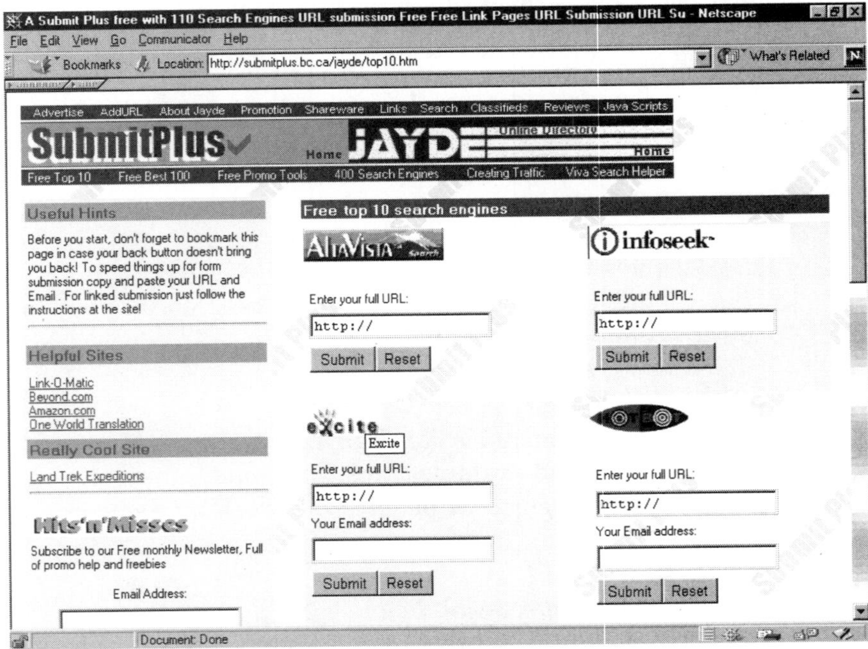

Figure 2.1. SubmitPlus is one of the multiple submission sites on the Net. From SubmitPlus you can submit to the best 100 search engines for free.

is completely free but requires some work on the submitter's part. Their second is a fee-based service where they do all the work for you and make sure your site content is ready for submission; this includes generating meta tags and producing mirror sites to get you on top of the most popular search engines. Before you register your site make sure you check out their Free Promotion Tools section for invaluable tips on how to make your web site ready for the Internet!

The Broadcaster
http://www.broadcaster.co.uk/
A free tool to list your site with the more important search engines and directories. Broadcaster will submit your URL (Internet address) to hundreds of search engines, directories, and link sites around the world.

MetaCrawlers Top Searches List
http://www.metaspy.com
Ever wonder what the rest of the world is searching for? Catch a glimpse of some of the searches being performed on MetaCrawler at this very moment!

WebStepTop 100
http://www.mmgco.com/4-star.html
This isn't a standard "link" site; it's much better than that. A listing of hundreds of search engines.

600+ Search Engine Submit
http://www.eyeonmedicine.com/dist/929088c.htm
This is a site with over 600 links to search engines, databases, directories, and yellow pages.

AAA Internet Promotions
http://www.web-ignite.com
One of the first professional web site promotion services on the Internet, and certainly the most reputable. AAA Internet Promotions manually submits your web site to search engines and directories. AAA also offers a Partner Program for webmasters and web site owners. Over 10,000 clients served include Price Waterhouse, AT&T, Sony Music, and Warner Brothers.

Web Themes Internet Consultants
http://www.webthemes.com
One of the most active submission and promotion services on the Net. They take a very active role in generating traffic to your site. For $200, they guarantee to get your site listed in the top 10 in InfoSeek. Web Themes Advertising, Marketing and Promotion and Design, home of The Web Hitman has been promoting new businesses on the web since 1995. They have experience and the resources to promote your Internet web site using a variety of tools to accomplish the task. Their web page promotion services start with your standard professional submission services and extend to extensive programs for increasing traffic on a daily basis.

Wilson Internet Services
http://www.wilsonweb.com/webmarket/
Dr. Wilson's Web Marketing Info Center is a "must visit" site. You'll find links to hundreds of online articles about effective Web marketing and resources for search engine and directory submission. From its beginning in August 1995, this site has become one of the most comprehensive Web marketing sites of its kind. It is a fantastic resource.

Jayde Online Directory
http://www.jayde.com/
The Jayde Online Directory offers a list of over 450 places to promote your site organized by type of directory. In addition, be sure to submit your site to the big site database maintained by Jayde.

Submit-It
http://www.submit-it.com
Very popular for site submission. Submit-it has a free submission engine that registers you in 20 places. If you want more, there is a fee-based service that lets you choose from hundreds of places to submit, and now there is a version that you can run on your desktop computer. Services include updates to the submission database for one year.

Business@merica
http://web.idirect.com/~tormall/links.html
A long list of 2,000 places to submit your site. Or with their Submission King, they will submit your URL to 500 search catalogs and directories for only 4 cents each. You get a full report on all those

that post your info. Their list includes the top 100 catalogs such as Alta Vista, Lycos, Webcrawler, Infoseek, Yahoo!, and hundreds of others worldwide.

The Web Hit Man
http://www.webthemes.com/hitman.html
The Hit Man is a site promotion service. They have a published list on their site of 500+ places to promote your site for the do-it-yourselfers. Look and see if they have any sites you have missed.

Eyescream Interactive
http://www.eyescream.com/yahootop200.html
A listing of Yahoo!'s top 200 search words.

Traffic Boost
http://www.inetexchange.com/unfair.htm
The Unfair Advantage submission service. Instantly submits your web site to 500 Internet search engines and directories.

The Net Submitter Pro
http://www.inetexchange.com/wps/
The Net Submitter Professional is the next generation of automated search engine submission tools. This client-side software product provides fully automated submission of unlimited URLs to a growing list of hundreds of search engines, directories, newsgroups, and link listings. In addition, semi-automated support is provided for hundreds of other submission sites.

Planetweb Broadcaster
http://www.broadcaster.co.uk/
Broadcaster will submit your URL (Internet Address) to hundreds of search engines, directories, and link sites around the world.

QuikLaunch Web Site Announcer
http://www.qwiklaunch.com/
A quick free way to get listed and launched in a number of popular search engines.

A1 Web Site Promotions
http://www.a1co.com//freeindex.html

Over 650 free WWW URL submission and search sites that will take your announcement.

SubmitWolf Pro
http://www.msw.com.au/swolf
With a database of over 1200 sites to promote your URL and 800+ fully automated submission scripts, SubmitWolf can dramatically increase your site traffic. SubmitWolf is loaded with features. It provides detailed submission reports, and it can generate meta tags to help search engines correctly index your site. It even enables you to add your own engines. Cost $65.

Dynamic Submission 2000 Version 4
http://www.submission2000.com/index1.html
This software program is a five-star award winning web site promotion tool. It will submit your web site (or URL) to 630+ major search engines with just a few button clicks. Enter your web site details and press a button. This program will automatically submit to hundreds of major search engines within minutes. On completion, it produces a full report for your records.

Site Success Station
http://www.etemp.com/station/?advance
You can submit your site to 300+ sources, help boost your site's rankings in search engines, learn insider site promotion techniques, and get advanced auditing of your site traffic.

Web Step Top 100 Promotion Sites
http://www.mmgco.com/4-star.html
The top 100 search engine and directory submission sites with information on how long it takes for your site to get listed, a start ranking on each of the top 100 sites, as well as a link to the submission form for each of the top 100.

Virtual Stampede
http://www.online-webstore.com/stampede/
Web site traffic building strategies, including free submission to top search engines.

3

Effective Promotional Use of Newsgroups

It is estimated that over 10 million people read newsgroups, making newsgroups an ideal marketing vehicle. The number of newsgroups is always increasing, with over 100,000 different topics now estimated. Using proper netiquette is important. To do this read the FAQs and rules, "lurk" first, and stay on topic. In this chapter we cover:

- The benefits of using newsgroups in your marketing plan
- Newsgroup netiquette
- Reading the FAQs, abiding by the rules, and lurking
- How to advertise if advertising is not allowed
- Developing your Usenet marketing strategy
- Identifying your target newsgroups
- Participating in this online community

- How to respond correctly to messages
- How to start your own newsgroup
- Cross posting and spamming
- Using Signature Files

Newsgroups—An Ideal Marketing Vehicle

News-groups
A discussion group on the Internet that focuses on a specific subject

It is estimated that over 10 million people read **newsgroups.** Usenet newsgroups are hierarchical and are arranged by subject. Each newsgroup is dedicated to a discussion of a particular topic, such as antique cars, home schooling, artificial intelligence, or The Spice Girls.

Usenet has been defined as follows:

> *"Usenet is the Internet's public forum, comprising thousands of newsgroups, each of which is devoted to the public discussion of a narrow, chartered topic such as microbrews, baseball cards, arthritis research, or travelling in Africa."*

Usenet facilitates the exchange of an abundance of information on every topic imaginable. Many newsgroups are tight-knit communities with very loyal residents.

Each group's readers are interested in the newsgroup topic and, therefore, when you find an appropriate newsgroup, you have found members of your target market. The number of newsgroups is steadily increasing. Currently it is estimated that there are more than 100,000 topics available. Different newsgroups have varying numbers of readers. Some are read by hundreds of thousands of readers a day, and others see very little traffic.

The newsgroup you decide to participate in may be read by a relatively small number of people or have a huge number of participants. Large isn't always better. A smaller group may provide you with a better chance of having your message read by your ideal target market. A larger group will provide you with better exposure by sheer volume. Whether you pick a large group or a small group depends on your objectives and also on your product or service.

For example, even though a posting to alt.politics may be seen by 300,000 readers, if what you are trying to sell is reproduction Model Ts, it will not likely generate more potential business than a posting to a Usenet group like *rec.antiquecars.misc* with only 1,000 readers. Not to mention that if your posting to alt.politics is inappropriate for that group, you will have done more harm than good. Newsgroup readers do not appreciate messages unrelated to their topic posted to their newsgroup, especially if these are advertisements.

If you use an online service, you can still participate in newsgroups because they have similar services. CompuServe has forums or special interest groups, AOL has forums and clubs, and Prodigy has forums and bulletin boards. The same rules regarding participation, acceptable messages, and marketing activities generally apply. Not only are newsgroups helpful marketing tools, but they can also help you identify competitors and trends in your industry, find valuable information from experts in your field, and assist you in the performance of market research activities.

The Benefits of Newsgroups

There are many ways online marketers can benefit from participating in newsgroups:

- **Reaching prospective customers:** You can immediately reach thousands of your targeted potential customers with a single message.

- **Communicating with existing customers:** You can provide your loyal customers with valuable information.

- **Market research:** You can use newsgroups to find out the latest trends, customer needs, what people are looking for, and what they are talking about.

- **Reputation building:** By answering people's questions and helping to solve their problems you will build your reputation as an expert in the field.

- **Increased Traffic:** You can direct people to your commercial web site if you do it in an informative way.

Thousands of Newsgroup Categories

Newsgroups are organized into different types of discussions or categories. Each of the major categories has hundreds of individual newsgroups in which you can participate. Major newsgroup categories include:

- **alt** Discussions on alternative topics
- **biz** Discussions on business topics. You may find groups that allow advertising here
- **comp** Discussions on computer related topics
- **misc** Discussions of miscellaneous topics that don't have their own category
- **news** Discussions on Usenet news and administration
- **rec** Discussions on recreation topics
- **sci** Discussions on science
- **soc** Discussions on social issues
- **talk** Making conversation

Target Appropriate Newsgroups

With the large number of Usenet newsgroups that currently exist, and the additional groups that are being introduced every day, it is a formidable task to identify appropriate newsgroups for your company's Internet marketing activities. First, you need to determine which newsgroups your prospective customers frequent.

Look for a close fit between a newsgroup and the product or service you are offering. For example, if your company sells software that aids genealogical work, then one appropriate newsgroup for your business might be soc.genealogy.methods. Try finding newsgroups that your target market may enjoy reading or ask your clients or customers which newsgroups they participate in or find particularly interesting. Find and make note of all appropriate newsgroups that might be of interest to your target customer.

There are many ways to find appropriate Usenet newsgroup listings: there are more than 54,000 mailing lists and newsgroups located at the Liszt Web Site, *http://www.liszt.com*. You can also do a search using the newsgroup functions of the two leading **browsers**, Netscape Navigator and Microsoft Internet Explorer. Be sure and check out Appendix B for more information on newsgroups.

Browsers
The software used to view the various kinds of Internet resources

Most newsreader programs have a search capability. Search the newsgroups for keywords that relate to your target market, your product, or your service to identify possible appropriate newsgroups for your marketing effort.

Another good place to start is Deja News, *http://www.dejanews.com*. At Deja News you can conduct a keyword search of the Usenet Newsgroups. The search results are displayed in chronological order, with the results at the top being the most recently used. You should choose keywords appropriate for your target customer or client. These methods will identify a fairly large list of potential newsgroups that may be included in your marketing activities.

If your company specializes in providing exotic vacations to Mexico, you may want to search Deja News for keywords like "Mexico, vacation, travel, tropical, resorts, beaches," and so on.

Once you have done your preliminary research and compiled a long list of what you think are the most appropriate newsgroups related to your target market, you are ready to investigate further and qualify your list.

The next step is to go to the Usenet Info Center Launch Pad at *http://sunsite.unc.edu/usenet-i/home.html*. There you can look up the newsgroups on your list. From this site you will be able to find out where the FAQs for each newsgroup are located. The FAQs will usually provide information on the newsgroup's stance on advertising. Info Center Launch Pad will also provide you with details on the number of people participating in the group.

Read the FAQs and Abide by the Rules

Charter
Established rules and guidelines

Read the FAQs, **charter**, and rules about posting and advertising for each of your target newsgroups. It is very important that you abide by all the rules. If the FAQs do not mention the group's stance on commercial advertising and announcements, then go back to Deja News. Conduct a search based on the group's name and charter. This will tell you where the newsgroup stands on commercial activity.

Lurking for Potential Customers

Lurking
Browsing without posting

Spend enough time **lurking** the newsgroup to determine if the participants of the newsgroup are, in fact, potential customers. Research the newsgroup to ascertain if it will appeal to your customers. The name of the newsgroup may not reveal what the newsgroup is about, so take your time and make sure.

Tips on Posting Messages

After you have become familiar with the rules of your selected newsgroup, have spent some time lurking, and have decided that the newsgroup is one where your target market is participating, you may begin to post messages. Remember to abide by the rules! If the rules do not allow advertising, then do not blatantly post an ad. To take full advantage of the newsgroup you have to gain the trust of its members. With one wrong message you could outrage all of the potential customers who participate in the newsgroup.

It is a good idea to run a test before you post a message to a newsgroup. Doing a test will show you how the posting works and prevent you from making a mistake when it comes to the real thing. For a test mechanism go to the newsgroup *misc.test*.

Becoming a respected member in a newsgroup is a way to promote yourself, as well as your company. In time you may forget that you began reading the newsgroup to promote your business. You will find yourself reading newsgroups in order to participate in stimulating discussions. You will be discussing anything and everything about the newsgroup subject. Only mention your web site when you find an appropriate opportunity to bring your business knowledge into the conversation.

Newsgroups exist for specific purposes. They can be designed for discussions, news announcements, postings related to particular topics, and even buying and selling goods.

Newsgroups may have hundreds of messages sorted and available for access at any point in time. Newsgroup participants will decide whether to open or pass your posted message based on the words in the subject area. Make your subject short and catchy so that your message will be read and not passed over. Try to put the most important words of the subject first. Some people adjust the screen to see only the first few words in the subject area. When deciding on the text for the subject area, think about what keywords someone would use to search for information on the content of your message.

Start your message with a short description on how it relates to the group's main topic. People are looking for answers to specific questions, so it is rude to jump into the conversation with a topic that doesn't match the one in the subject line.

Message length should be short, no longer than 24 lines. Messages should briefly discuss main points and ask if readers would like to have more information. Once people show an interest in the information you are offering, your message can be as long as needed.

When responding to a message in a newsgroup, you have the option of responding to the individual who posted the message privately or responding through the newsgroup. Determine which is more appropriate under the given circumstances. If your message will be of value to the entire group or will appropriately promote your company's capabilities, then post the response to the newsgroup for all to see. If you think that your company has a solution for the individual and would like to provide details to the "target customer," but feel that it would not benefit the other members of the group, then deliver a private response. Whichever approach you take, make sure that you respond as quickly as possible so that the first message is still fresh in the mind of the recipient.

Tips to Ensure Your Messages Will be Well Received

Here are some basic rules to help you post well-received messages:

Keep to the newsgroup topic

Make sure to always stay on the newsgroup topic of discussion. People participate in specific newsgroups because of that subject and don't appreciate off-topic postings.

Stay on the thread

When responding to a message, use the reply option to stay on the same thread. Summarize the parts of the original message that you are responding to for the benefit of the readers—do not include the entire message.

Make a contribution

Informed quality responses to people's questions will give you credibility with the group and reflect well upon you and your company.

Don't post commercials

Advertising is not welcome in most newsgroups, and many charters specifically disallow the posting of ads. Read the FAQs before posting a message.

You don't have to have the last word

Don't post gratuitous responses in newsgroups. Never post a message with just a "Thanks" or "I like it" if you have nothing else to contribute. If you feel such a response is warranted or would like to discuss the issue privately, send a private e-mail to the person to convey your appreciation or opinion.

Signature Files as your e-Business Card

Signature file
An e-business card usually attached to e-mail

A **signature file**, or sig. file as it is commonly referred to, is your e-business card. It is a short message at the end of an e-mail. Most, if not all, e-mail programs allow for the use of a signature file. Sig.files can be attached at the end of your message when you post to a Usenet newsgroup or a mailing list, even if the group does not allow advertising.

You can use your sig.file in a number of clever ways. Sig.files can be simple—only listing phone numbers and addresses—or they can be a virtual ad for your company. They can be very useful in providing exposure for your company. You can use your sig.file to offer some substantial information, like letting people know about a special event, informing people about an award or honor your company has received, or promoting a specific product or service your company has to offer.

You can design and use different sig.files for posting to different newsgroups. A particular sig.file may be appropriate for one newsgroup but not for another. Always ensure that the message in your sig.file is appropriate for its audience.

Keep your sig.file short. Usually 4 to 8 lines is a good size. There is nothing more annoying than a sig.file that is longer than the text of your message to which it is attached, or one that resembles a brochure.

Sig.files should include the following:

- Contact name
- Business name
- URL
- Address
- Email address

- Telephone number
- Fax number
- A brief company tag line or a company slogan

This is an example of what a sig.file looks like:

Jane Doe, Marketing Assistant
jdoe@bug.com
Sunnyvale Volkswagen
101 Main Street
Woodstock, NY, 10010
Toll Free Tel: (800) 555-1001 Fax: (800) 555-1000
"www.bug.com"

For a complete discussion of sig. files and how to use them see Chapter 4.

Newsgroup Advertising Hints

Newsgroups have been developed for different audiences and different topics. There are some newsgroups that are dedicated to posting advertisements. If advertising is appropriate for your company, the following newsgroup types might be included in your Internet marketing strategy. Most of the newsgroups that allow advertising are readily identifiable. The newsgroup name itself might include one of the following:

- biz
- classified
- for sale
- marketplace

Again, read the FAQs and lurk to determine if the newsgroup is appropriate for your target market before you post. Use a short catchy subject line with keywords at the beginning—the subject will determine whether your message warrants a read or a pass. Avoid CAPITALS. This is equivalent to shouting on the Internet. Stay away from !!!!, ****, and @@@@ and other such symbols.

When you have found a newsgroup whose participants include your target market but the newsgroup does not allow advertising, don't despair. By responding to queries or providing information that is of genuine interest to the newsgroup, you have the opportunity to attach your sig. file. A sig. file can be as effective as an ad if it is designed properly. Your message should offer substantial information to the discussion (a thinly veiled excuse to get your sig. file posted will not be appreciated). If your information is relevant and of value to the participants of the newsgroup, the fact that your sig. file is an advertisement will not matter—in fact it may add credibility to the information you have provided and enhance your company's reputation.

Cross Posting and Spamming

Cross posting is when someone posts identical messages to a number of relevant newsgroups. Doing this is considered to be inappropriate because of the number of common users in associated newsgroups. Spamming is when you post identical or nearly identical messages to irrelevant newsgroups without care or regard for the posting guidelines, the newsgroup topic, or the interests of the group. Cross posting and spamming will annoy the readers of the newsgroup. Doing these things will reflect badly on you and your company, and prevent you from achieving your online marketing objectives.

Sometime in your online postings, no matter how careful you are, someone is bound to get upset. Accept this as fact and learn how to handle flames appropriately. Be sensitive to complaints. Learn from them, but do not worry unnecessarily. If someone posts a message that reflects badly on your company, you have three options: defend your comments in the newsgroup, send the person a private e-mail, or do nothing. Responding to the person via e-mail is the most appropriate response, even though in most cases your message will be ignored.

Earning Respect with Newsgroup Netiquette

Following are ten rules for Netiquette. Incorporating them in your newsgroup posting will gain you respect by the other participants:

1. Don't use CAPITALS. CAPS are akin to shouting on the Internet.
2. Don't post ads where they are not welcome.
3. Do provide valuable, on-topic information for the newsgroup.
4. Don't be rude or sarcastic.
5. Don't include the entire message you are replying to in your response. Only quote relevant sections of the original message.
6. Do a thorough review of your message before you post. Check your spelling and grammar. Check your subject; it should be short and catchy with the keywords first.
7. Do provide an appropriate sig. file.
8. Don't post messages that are too lengthy. Online communication tends to be one screen or less.
9. Don't spam or cross post.
10. Don't post replies that contribute nothing to the discussion ("I agree" or "Thanks").

Have Your Own Newsgroup

You can start your own newsgroup if you feel it is warranted and appropriate. All group creation requests must follow set guidelines and are first met with discussion. If you need help, you can always find a body of volunteers who are experienced in the newsgroup creation process at group-*mentors@acpub.duke.edu*. They assist people with the formation and submission of good newsgroup proposals.

The Discussion

A request for discussion on creation of a new newsgroup should be posted to news.announce.newsgroups and news.groups. If desired, the request can also be posted to other groups or mailing lists that are related to the proposed topic. The name and charter of the proposed group and whether it will be moderated or unmoderated should be determined during the discussion period.

The Vote

The Usenet Volunteer Vote Takers (UVT) is a group of neutral third-party vote-takers who currently handle vote gathering and counting for all newsgroup proposals. There should be a minimal delay between the end of the discussion period and the issuing of a call for votes. The call for votes should include clear instructions on how to cast a vote. The voting period should last for at least 21 days and no more than 31days. Only the votes that are mailed to the vote taker will be counted.

The Result

At the completion of the voting period, the vote taker must post the vote tally to the applicable groups and mailing lists. The Email addresses and names (if available) of the voters are posted along with the tally. There will be a five-day waiting period, beginning when the voting results actually appear. During the waiting period there will be a chance to correct any errors in the voter list or the voting procedure. In order for a proposal to pass, 100 more YES/create votes must be received than NO/do not create votes. Also, 2/3 of the total number of votes must be in favor of creation. If a proposal fails to achieve 2/3 of the vote, then the matter cannot be brought up for discussion until at least six months have passed from the close of the vote.

The following locations will help you should you wish to create your own newsgroup:

- How to Format and Submit a New Group Proposal: *news.announce.newgroups, news.groups*
- How to Write a Good Newsgroup Proposal: *news.announce.newgroups, news.groups*
- Usenet Newsgroup Creation Companion:*news.groups, news.announce.newusers, news.answers*

Internet Resources for Chapter 3

Newsgroups
News.newusers.questions
News.announce.newusers
News.newusers
These provide information to new Usenet users on posting, finding appropriate newsgroups, netiquette, and other frequently asked questions new users are faced with.

Reference.COM Search
http://www.reference.com
Reference.com has searchable directories of newsgroups and mailing lists. Newsgroups are archived, but mailing lists are only archived and searchable with the permission of the list owner.

Deja News - The Source for Internet Newsgroups!
http://www.dejanews.com
The web site where you can read, search, participate in, and subscribe to more than 50,000 discussion forums, including Usenet newsgroups. Deja News is a resource for finding people, getting noticed, and getting answers to all sorts of questions. You can find discussion forums on any topic imaginable.

The Last Internet Gold Rush
http://www.thestandard.net/articles/article_display/0,1449,1304,00.html
Nineteen years after its creation, Usenet may be experiencing a renaissance. Long the web's overlooked sibling, it's now seeing a surge in interest with online communities hot in the investment world.

Liszt of Newsgroups
http://www.liszt.com/news
A complete listing of newsgroups organized by different categories. Has listed over 30,000 newsgroups and is the largest directory of newsgroups on the web.

How to Advertise on Newsgroups
http://www.nsmi.com/noflames.html
How to Advertise on Newsgroups shows step-by-step techniques to follow so you won't get blacklisted. Everything you need to know about how to advertise in newsgroups and mailing lists without getting flamed.

Creating Newsgroups
http://www.fairnet.org/fnvol/training/newsgrp.html
All you need to know about how to create your own newsgroup.

Public news servers
http://login.eunet.no/~kjetilm/news.htm
Free access to newsgroups/NNTP servers.

Open Newsserver Search
http://www.muenz.com/sdienst/html/sgroup_e.html
English/German search engine that finds open newsservers that carry newsgroups matching your search terms.

Newsgroups
http://www.engl.uvic.ca/OnlineGuide/News/newsGroupsWel.html
Introductory information called the Online Guide.

NIC - Master List
http://sunsite.unc.edu/usenet-i/hier-s/master.html
See this master list for a descriptions of newsgroups.

Usenet Tools and Tips
http://netscan.sscnet.ucla.edu
Netscan Home Statistics concerns itself with the creation of, and activity in, Usenet newsgroups.

Locations of the Blacklist of Internet Advertisers
http://math-www.uni-paderborn.de/~axel/blacklist.html
This is a guide about how *not* to get attention online!

Downloading Free Agent
http://www.forteinc.com/getfa/getfa.htm
Free Agent furnishes newsreader software.

Talkway
http://www.talkway.com
This membership site attempts to provide a friendlier interface to the arcane structure of Usenet newsgroups.

SIFT Netnews server at Stanford University
http://www.stanford.edu
Sift Netnews provides, via e-mail, a personalized news delivery service. After you subscribe online you can submit details on the subject you are interested in, and SIFT will e-mail you newsgroup postings that meet your criteria.

4

Utilizing Signature Files to Increase Web Site Traffic

A signature file is a short memo at the end of your message. You can use your signature file in a number of clever ways, from just giving out phone numbers and addresses, to offering some substantial information. Sig. files can be used to let people know about a special event or to inform people about an award or honor you company has received. In this chapter we cover:

- The appropriate size of sig. files
- Content and design of sig. files
- Creating signature files to add statements to your messages
- The benefits of sig. files

Presenting Your e-Business Card

A signature file, or sig.file as it is commonly referred to, is your e-business card. It should be attached at the end of all your e-mails, those that are sent to individuals and especially those that are sent to Usenet newsgroups and mail lists.

Most, if not all e-mail programs, allow for the use of a signature file. If yours doesn't, you should consider switching e-mail programs because sig. files can be very effective in drawing traffic to your web site when used appropriately.

You can use your sig.file in a number of different ways, from providing the basic contact information such as phone, fax, e-mail and URL details to offering more substantial information about your company and its products and services. You can tell your readers about a current sales promotion, where you will be located at a trade show, a special event you are hosting, or an award your company has received. Sig.files are readily accepted online and, when designed properly, comply with netiquette.

How to Develop Your Signature File

Tag Line
Advertising message usually included in your signature file card attached to e-mail

In preparation for designing and developing your sig. file, you should decide what information you want to include and what you want your e-business card to look like. Create your sig.file using Windows Notepad and save it as a text file (that's with a .txt extension). After you have developed your sig. file, send an e-mail message to yourself with it attached to see what it looks like. Make sure to check and double check for typos, errors, or omissions.

One of the most important elements from a marketing perspective is the **tag line**. Does your tag line give the reader a real and compelling desire to visit your web site?

If you are using one of the online services, there are different ways to develop your sig.file:

- **America Online:**

  1. Enter keyword "newsgroups"

  2. Choose "set preferences"

  3. Type your sig. file information in the signature box

4. When posting a message, select "use signature box" at the bottom

- **CompuServe:**

1. Click the "special" button
2. Choose "preferences"
3. Click on "general"
4. Click on "set function keys"
5. Enter the name of your sig.file in the "key definition box"
6. Click "ok"

- **Prodigy:**

1. Click on the "edit pull down menu"
2. Select "scratch pad"
3. Type in your sig. file
4. Save it with a .mac extension (macro)
5. When you want to post a message and you want to use your sig.file, select "play macros" from the "goodies" menu and your sig.file will be attached to your message.

The Dos and Don'ts of Signature Files

It is a good idea to develop several signature files to use with different groups of recipients. You can use an appropriate sig.file for each different group you are targeting. You should update your sig.file often to reflect current marketing related information.

Some e-mail programs allow a maximum of 80 characters per line for sig.files. You should design your sig. file to fit well within the limits of all programs. Use no more than 70 characters per line to be assured that your sig. file will be viewed as you have designed it no matter what reader is being used.

Some people get really innovative in the design of their sig.files. They often include sketches, designs, or logos developed by combining keyboard numbers and punctuation. An example of this is "John Doe" of "Game Corporation." They are in the game software business.

```
>>>>>>>>>>>>>>>>>>>>>>>>>>>>>>>>>>>>>>>>>>>>>>>>>>>>>
John Doe, Director of Marketing                  jdoe@gamecorp.com
                                                 Tel: (800) 555-0008
 _________
| GAME CORP |                                    Fax: (800) 555-0009
|   ______  |                                       290 Young St.
| |       | |        "Free Trial Version @          New York, NY
|_|__||||___|_|       www.gamecorp.com"                  81010
GAME CORP.
>>>>>>>>>>>>>>>>>>>>>>>>>>>>>>>>>>>>>>>>>>>>>>>>>>>>>
```

Including graphics in your sig.file may be appropriate for certain types of businesses but definitely not all. If you have designed one of these innovative sig.files but are not sure if it is appropriate, get a second opinion and maybe a third.

Check out sig.files attached to messages you receive or those posted to newsgroups to see what you like, what you don't, and what suits you best. You can always build it, test it on your colleagues, and then decide whether you will use it or not.

The use of signature files offers a number of benefits to your company. If you use sig. files appropriately, you will be able to promote your company and your online presence in the following ways.

- The use of sig. files will increase your company's online exposure. By merely placing a sig. file at the end of a posting to a newsgroup, your company name may be seen by thousands of people. A great tag line with a call to action will encourage people to visit your site.

- Like any advertisement, the design and content of your sig. file can be used to position your business and create or complement a corporate image.

- Using your sig. file can enhance the reputation of your company based upon the e-mail that it is attached to. If your postings to newsgroups and mailing lists are helpful and continually appreciated, this will become associated with your company name.

- Using appropriate sig. files, as shown below, will signal to the online community that you are a member that respects proper netiquette.

Sig.file DOs	Sig.file DON'Ts
Do list all appropriate contact information	Don't list prices of any kind
Keep it short, say 4 to 8 lines	Don't use a sales pitch
Keep it simple	Don't use too many symbols
Provide an appropriate and professional tag line	Don't list the company's products or service

Sig. Files to Bring Traffic to Your Web Site

The major benefit of sig. files is that they can attract visitors to your web site. Use your signature file as an advertisement for your company and its products and services. With sigvertising you can go beyond offering the basic contact information. Use your sig. file as a tool to bring traffic to your web site. Instead of simply listing your company's phone number and URL, give the reader some insight into your company and a reason to visit your web site. Use some of the following tips to increase the traffic to your web site:

- **Announce a sale or special offer.** Briefly mention that your company will be having a sale, or inform people that there is a special offer available on your web site.

- **Offer something for free.** Inform readers of free information or samples that they can access if they visit your site.

- **Announce an event.** If your company is organizing or sponsoring a special event, inform people through your sig. file, and invite them to your site for more information.

- **Announce a contest.** If your site is holding a contest tell readers that they can enter by visiting your site.

- **Announce an award or honor.** If your company or your web site has received special recognition, tell people about it through your sig. file.

Sig. files are accepted online in e-mail, newsgroups, mail lists, and discussion groups. However, be cautious when developing your sig. files to ensure that they will be well received. Sig. files that are billboards, or sig. files that are longer than most of your text messages, are to be avoided. Sig.files that are blatant advertisements will definitely not be appreciated. The online community reacts unfavorably to hard-sell advertising unless it is done in the proper forum. Here is an example of a sig.file that may offend Internet users.

xxxxxxxxxxxxxxxxxxxxxxxxxxxxxxxxxxxxxxxxxxxxxxxxxxxxxxxxxxxxxxxxxxxxxxxxxxxx

Are you in need of a reliable vehicle?
If you are, come on down to Sunnyvale Volkswagen!
We have the best deals in town and will beat any of our
competitor's prices on new and used cars!
Money back guarantee!
Great deal on a 1995 Diesel Jetta.....$ 2995.
Talk to Jane Doe about our new lease incentives!
101 Main Street, Woodstock
New York 10010
Tel: (800) 555-0000
Cell: (800) 555-1010
Fax: (800) 555-1020
www.bug.com

xxxxxxxxxxxxxxxxxxxxxxxxxxxxxxxxxxxxxxxxxxxxxxxxxxxxxxxxxxxxxxxxxxxxxxxxxxxx

Another mistake that people make is that they try to make their sig.files too flashy or eye catching. Using a lot of large symbols may catch people's eye, but the impression it leaves will not be memorable. Here is an example of what not to do.

☯☺☺☺✉☺☺☺✉☺☺☺✉☺☺☺✉☺☺☺✉☺☺☺✉☺☺☺✉☺☺☺✉☺☺☺☯
☯ **! Sunnyvale Volkswagen !** ☯
☯ **! Jane Doe, Marketing Assistant !** ☯
☯ **! jdoe@bug.com !** ☯
☯ 232 Main Street ☎ (800) 555-0000 ☯
☯ Woodstock, New York (800) 555-0002 ☯
☯ 30210 ☯
☯ **"Test drives @ www.bug.com"** ☯
☯☺☺☺✉☺☺☺✉☺☺☺✉☺☺☺✉☺☺☺✉☺☺☺✉☺☺☺✉☺☺☺✉☺☺☺☯

Here are some examples of what sig. files should look like.

===

Sunnyvale Volkswagen
Jane Doe, Marketing Assistant
jdoe@bug.com
101 Main Street Tel: (800) 555-0000
Woodstock, New York ,10010 Fax:(800) 555-0002
"Our once a year sales event is on now @ www.bug.com"

===

♦♦♦
Jane Doe, Marketing Assistant **Sunnyvale Volkswagen**
jdoe@bug.com
101 Main Street Tel: (800) 555-0000
Woodstock, New York,10010 Fax: (800) 555-0001

♦♦♦♦♦♦♦♦♦♦♦♦♦♦♦♦♦♦♦♦♦♦♦♦♦♦♦♦♦♦♦♦♦♦♦
Charity Telethon sponsored by Sunnyvale Volkswagen
info available @ www.bug.com
♦♦♦

Jane Doe * Marketing Assistant * Sunnyvale Volkswagen

"Enter to win a new 1999 Bug @ www.bug.com"

101 Main Street, Woodstock, New York, 10010
(800) 555-0000 jdoe@bug.com

\>>>

Jane Doe, Marketing Assistant
Sunnyvale Volkswagen

101 Main Street jdoe@bug.com
P. O. Box 101 Tel: (800) 555-0000
Woodstock, New York 10010 URL: www.bug.com
"1999 Winner of the Best Dealership Award"

\>>>

Jane Doe, Marketing Assistant **jdoe@bug.com**
Sunnyvale Volkswagen
101 Main Street Tel: (800) 500-1000
P.O. Box 101 Fax: (800) 500-1002
Woodstock, NY 10010 URL: www.bug.com
"Test Drives @ www.bug.com"

Internet Resources for Chapter 4

123 Promote
http://www.123promote.com/workbook/plan1.htm
E-mail guide to e-mail styles, e-mail mail-merging, e-mail auto responders, e-mail auto reminders, e-mail netiquette, e-mail headers, signature files, announcements, press releases, business administra-

tion, free designs, mailing list announcements, newsgroup announcements, office automation, mass e-mailing, publicity, form letters, form folders, e-mailed databases, programs, software.

Internet Strategist
http://www.techdirect.com/strategy/sigfiles.html
What to do and not do on sig. files and mailing lists. Learn how to create your personal sig. file and what the different types are used for.

SquareOne Technology: How to create an e-mail signature?
http://www.squareonetech.com/signatur.html
How to create a sig.file with Notepad and import it to use with all your mail messages.

Signature Files
http://www.smithfam.com/news/n8.html
Signature files are an absolutely vital way of promoting your web site. Learn how to market your product on the Internet from the leading Internet marketing experts, and it is all free.

GFOFN Help: How to Make and Maintain a Signature File
http://www.gnofn.org/info/help/ppp/makesig.html
A tutorial on designing and developing your signature file.

Esther's Massive Signature File Collection
http://www.contrib.andrew.cmu.edu/~moose/sigs.html
A massive collection of sig. files to review the good, the bad, and the ugly.

32bit.com
http://www.32bit.com/hyper95/get/internet/798.html
A tutorial on adding links in signature files in Netscape 3.x and 4.x.

Signature Museum
http://huizen.dds.nl/~mwpieter/sigs/
The Signature Museum is a gallery of signature files sorted by category. At this site you will also find a list of other sites that provide examples of lots and lots of signature files.

5

The E-mail Advantage

E-mail is rapidly becoming the most crucial form of communication you have with your clients, potential customers, suppliers, and colleagues. E-mail is now a widely accessible and generally accepted form of communication. In the online community e-mail is an extremely efficient way to build and maintain relationships. As a marketing tool, e-mail is one of the most cost-effective ways to maintain an ongoing dialogue with your audience. In this chapter we cover:

- Strategies for creating effective e-mail messages
- E-mail netiquette
- How to use private mailing lists for prospective clients and customers
- How to assemble appropriate e-mail lists
- Purchasing e-mail lists or online mail services
- Information access with autoresponders

Making the Connection

E-mail is a communication medium, and, as with all forms of communication, *you do not get a second chance to leave a first impression.* E-mail must be used appropriately. People receive large amounts of e-mail each day and the tips in this chapter will help to ensure that your e-mail is taken seriously.

One of the greatest benefits of e-mail is the speed with which you can communicate. E-mail takes seconds rather than weeks to send a message around the world. The cost of this form of communication is negligible compared to making a long distance phone call or sending a fax. The economies of scale are significant, as one e-mail message can be sent to millions of people across the globe simultaneously. This type of mass mailing is done at a fraction of the cost and a fraction of the time (and internal resources) it would take with **snail mail.**

All kinds of files can be sent via e-mail including sound, video, data, graphics, and text. With **autoresponders**, information can be sent to customers and potential customers 24 hours a day, 7 days a week, 365 days a year in response to their online requests.

Snail Mail
Slang term for the regular postal service

Effective E-mail Messages

Most people who use this medium get tons and tons of e-mail, including their share of junk e-mail. The following tips will increase the effectiveness of your e-mail communication.

Autoresponder
Program that automatically responds to incoming e-mail. An electronic fax-back system

The Importance of Your E-mail Subject Line

The subject line is equivalent to a headline in a newspaper in terms of attracting reader attention. It is the most important part of your e-mail message as this phrase alone will determine whether or not the reader will decide to open your e-mail or delete it.

When you receive e-mails, what do you use to determine which e-mail to read first or at all? The subject line of course! Never send an e-mail without a subject line. Subject lines should be brief with the keywords appearing first. The longer the subject line, the more likely it will not be viewed in entirety.

Effective subject lines will:

- Be brief, yet capture the reader's interest
- Build business credibility
- Attract attention with action words
- Highlight the most important benefits
- Always be positive
- Put the most important words first

Effective headlines should grab the reader's attention, isolate, and qualify your best prospects, and draw your reader into the sub-headlines and the text itself. Remember to avoid SHOUTING! Using CAPITALS in your subject is the same as SHOUTING AT THE READER! DON'T DO IT!!

E-mail To and From Headings Allow You to Personalize

Use personal names in the *To* and *From* headings whenever possible as this creates a more personal relationship. Most e-mail programs allow you to attach your personal name to your e-mail address. If you don't know how to do this, look at the help file of the e-mail program you are using.

BCC
Blind carbon copy

It is advisable to use the BCC feature when sending bulk e-mails; otherwise every person on the list will see that this e-mail was not sent just to him or her. The e-mail recipients will see the list of the other recipients first and not the intended message. They will be required to scroll down past the list of recipients to get to your message. This is not the best way to "make friends and influence people." Make sure that you know how to use the blind carbon copy function in your e-mail program.

Before you send any "live" bulk e-mail, do a test with a number of your colleagues and friends to make sure you are using the program and features effectively and that all of their addresses do not appear by mistake in each message.

Effective E-mail Message Formatting

The content of the message should be focused on one topic. If you need to change the subject in the middle of a message, it is better to send a separate e-mail. E-mail is similar to writing a business letter in that the spelling and grammar should be correct. However, e-mail is unlike a business letter in that the tone is completely different. E-mail correspondence is not as formal as business writing. The *tone* of e-mail is more similar to a polite conversation than a formal letter.

- Keep your paragraphs relatively short—no more than 7 lines.
- Make your point in the first paragraph.
- Be clear and concise.
- Give your reader a call to action.
- Keep each line between 65 and 70 characters to ensure that it is viewed correctly.
- Avoid using fancy formatting such as: graphics, different fonts, italics, and bold since many e-mail programs cannot display those features. Your e-mail will most likely be unreadable where these features occur.
- If your e-mail package doesn't have a spell check feature, you might want to consider composing your message first in your

word processing program. Spell check it there and then cut and paste it into your e-mail package.

- If you want to be really careful, test the e-mail in a number of the popular packages to ensure your message will be received in the intended format.

Appropriate E-mail Reply Tips

Download Transmission of a file from one computer to another

Do not include the entire original message in your replies. This is unnecessary, aggravating the original sender of the message, and it often takes too long to **download**. Use only enough of the original message to refresh the recipient's memory. Remember to check the *To* and CC before you reply. You would not want an entire mail list to receive your response intended only for the sender. The same applies for selecting *Reply All* instead of *Reply*.

Always Use Your Signature Files

As discussed previously, signature files are a great marketing tool. Always attach your signature file to your online communication. (See Chapter 4 on Signature Files.)

Discerning Use of Attachments

If you are sending a fairly large volume of data, send it as an attachment file to your e-mail message. Use ASCII text (.txt) format. Unless the recipient of your e-mail is expecting it, don't send an attachment that is larger than 50k.

Viruses Programs that contaminate

Never send lengthy, unsolicited file attachments. It aggravates and angers most recipients when they retrieve their e-mail messages and find a message with a lengthy file attached that they did not request (or want), which may take an inordinate amount of time to download and is now stored on their hard drive (with or without attached **viruses**).

Before You Click on Send

There are a number of things you should do before you send an important e-mail, especially if it is going to a number of people. Send a test message to yourself or a colleague so that you can check that the word wrap looks good and that the text is formatted properly, displaying as you want it to. Check that there are no typos, errors, or omissions.

Expressing Yourself with Emoticons and Shorthand

In verbal communication you provide details on your mood, meaning, and intention through voice inflections, tone and volume. You also give clues about your meaning and intention through facial expression and body language. E-mail does not allow for the same expression of feeling. The closest thing we have to this online is the use of **emoticons**.

The word "emoticons" is an acronym for "emotions" and "icons." Emoticons are combinations of keyboard characters that give the appearance of a stick figure's emotions. They have to be viewed sideways and are meant to be smiling, frowning, laughing, etc. Emoticons let you communicate your meaning and intentions to your reader.

Emoticons Symbols made from punctuation marks and letters that look like facial expressions

For example if your boss gives you an assignment via e-mail and your response is, "Thanks a lot for unloading your dirty work on me," your boss may become upset at your obvious defiance. But if you replied with this: "Thanks a lot for unloading your dirty work on me :-)," your boss would understand that you were jokingly accepting the assignment.

Emoticons enable you to add a little personality and life to your text messages. However, their use is not universal and should generally not be used in business correspondence.

Some of the more commonly used emoticons are:

:-)	Smiling	:-0	Wow!
;-)	Wink	:-V	Shout
;-) or ;-<	Crying	:-&	Tongue tied

:-*	Ooops!	8-0	No Way!
:-<	Sad or frown	%-0	Bug-eyed
:-D	Laughing, big smile	:-@	Screaming
:-p	Tongue wagging	(-:	I'm left handed
:-o	Wow!	:-r	Tongue hanging out
:-#	My lips are sealed!	:-S	I'm totally confused
:-/	Skeptical	~~:-(	just got flamed!

E-mail shorthand is used in newsgroups and other e-mail to represent commonly used phrases. Some common abbreviations are:

- BTW – By the way
- IMHO – In my humble opinion
- IMO – In my opinion
- IOW – In other words
- JFYI – Just for your information
- NBD – No big deal
- NOYB – None of your business
- TIA – Thanks in advance
- PMFJI – Pardon me for jumping in
- OIC – Oh, I see...
- OTL – Out to lunch
- OTOH – On the other hand
- LOL – laughing out loud
- LMHO – Laughing my head off
- ROFL – Rolling on the floor laughing

- BFN – Bye for now
- CYA – See ya!
- FWIW – For what it's worth
- IAE – In any event
- BBL – Be back later
- BRB – Be right back
- RS – Real soon
- TIC – Tongue in cheek
- TTFN – Ta-ta for now
- TTYL – talk to you later
- TWF – That was fun
- YMBJ – You must be joking!
- WYSIWYG – What you see is what you get
- <g> – Adding a grin

Since e-mail shorthand is most commonly used in newsgroups and chatrooms, you will be most successful when using these acronyms with others who are familiar with them.

Using Automated Mail Responders—Mailbots and Infobots

Automated mail responders act like fax-back systems. They send requested information via e-mail automatically to the person that made the request. You can ask your Internet Service Provider (ISP) for details on autoresponder services they may offer. Alternatively, you can also do a search on "mailbots" to find any third-party companies that can provide you with one of these services.

You can make information on your company, your products, and services, and your marketing materials easily accessible 24 hours a day, 7 days a week, 365 days a year through mailbots. Examples of information that you can easily provide through this service are:

- Catalogue and price lists
- Brochures
- Reviews and testimonials
- Press releases
- Newsletters
- Annual reports
- Award announcements
- Sample reports

E-mail Marketing Tips

You will receive a number of e-mails requesting information on your company, your products, your locations, etc., from people who have seen your e-mail address on letterhead, ads, business cards and sig. files. Be prepared to respond by following these tips:

Brochure and Personal Note

Have an electronic brochure available that you can easily access and send via e-mail. Try to send a personal note in your e-mail along with any material requested.

Gather a Library of Responses

You will have different people asking a number of the same questions, and over time you will be able to develop a library of responses to these frequently asked questions. You can save a lot of time by copying and pasting the answers to FAQs into your e-mail responses. Again, always make sure to personalize your responses.

Have More Than One E-mail Box

By having a number of different e-mail boxes you can develop databases of all the people who have sent you a message—sorted by their interests. (You will know their interests by which mailbox they choose to send an e-mail to.) For example, you may be able to tell that a person is interested in your virus scanners but not your game software, or that they were interested in your information on making animated .gifs but not on your virus archive.

The tactic of using different mailboxes can be used for many marketing purposes other than developing e-mail lists. For example, you can promote different mailboxes with different advertisements so that you can track the number and quality of responses from various types of advertising or different publications.

Following Formalities with E-mail Netiquette

When writing e-mails remember to:

- Be courteous...remember your please and thank-yous
- Reply promptly...within 24 hours
- Be brief
- Use lowercase characters. Capitals indicate SHOUTING!
- Use emoticons where appropriate

- Check your grammar and spelling
- Use attachments sparingly

Internet Resources for Chapter 5

E-mail Netiquette
http://ultra.santarosa.edu/net/email/netiquette.html
This document is from David Harris, author of Pegasus Mail, a popular PC and MAC e-mail package to help get the most from your e-mail.

E-mail Netiquette
http://www.vtt.fi/cic/links/netiquet.html
The growing volume of e-mail is becoming difficult to manage. Receivers want to be able to sort/filter messages according to context. They may not have time to read all incoming e-mail and may want to decide whether to read or delete a message before opening it.

The Marketing Advantage of E-mail
http://home.att.net/~b..ford/awwartmarademail.htm
An article on the benefits and what to do for sending business by electronic mail in order to receive the most business.

Everything E-mail
http://everythingemail.net/
Information and links to make your e-mail account more productive and fun! Resources, guides, and glossary to make things easier for you to understand. Extensive Web site dedicated exclusively to e-mail and e-mail services.

123 Promote
http://www.123promote.com/workbook/plan1.htm
E-mail guide to e-mail styles, mail-merging, auto responders, auto reminders, netiquette, headers, signature files, announcements, press releases, business administration, free designs, mailing list announcements, newsgroup announcements, office automation, mass e-mailing, publicity, form letters, form folders, e-mailed databases, programs, and software.

A Beginner's Guide to Effective E-mail
http://www.webfoot.com/advice/email.top.html
Help in writing the e-mail you need. Formats and why you need e-mail is all explained in detail.

Neophyte's Guide to Effective E-mail
http://www.webnovice.com/email.htm
This site goes through, step-by-step, the important issues you should keep in mind from start to send.

Internet E-mail Marketing
http://www.smithfam.com/email.html
Fantastic resource with information and links to many e-mail marketing information and tools. Lists and links of free e-mail resources, lists of lists, services, autoresponders, and newsgroups for marketers.

Internet Marketing Newsletter
http://www.arrowweb.com/graphics/news/ap12.html
"The Secrets of E-mail Marketing Success," an article by Lesley Anne Lowe.

Windweaver
http://www.windweaver.com/emoticon.htm
Recommended emoticons for e-mail communication.

Dave Barry's Guide to Emoticons
http://www.randomhouse.com/features/davebarry/emoticon.html
Good resource for emoticons and shorthand. His site has an Emoticon Gallery with lots of examples (3069 at last count) and an area where you can make your own.

EEF's Extended Guide to the Internet
http://www.eff.org/papers/eegtti/eeg_286.html
This *Unofficial Smiley Dictionary* is only one of many different collections by various "editors" you'll come across at many places on the Net.

Aaron's Emoticons
http://www.teleport.com/~rhubarbs/faces.htm
Another extensive source of emoticons.

6

Effective Mailing List Promotion

Internet mailing lists are quick and easy ways to distribute information to a large number of people. There are thousands of publicly available online lists. You can also create your own Internet mailing lists to keep your clients and prospects informed of company events, product announcements, and press releases. In this chapter we cover:

- How to identify appropriate mailing lists
- Subscribing to the mailing list
- Writing messages that will be read
- Mailing list netiquette
- Creating your own mailing list

Connecting with Your Target Audience

Mailing lists are publicly available lists of e-mail addresses that can be accessed and used to send e-mail to targeted groups online. They are organized by subject matter in a way similar to Usenet newsgroups. And, likewise, the size of each mailing list varies. People subscribe to particular lists to participate in that list and receive all of the postings that are sent to the group, generally because they have an interest in the topic. When you post a message to a mailing list, the message is sent out to everyone who has subscribed to the list by e-mail.

Internet mailing lists are quick and easy ways to distribute information to a large number of people interested in a particular topic. The difference between mailing lists and newsgroups is that anyone on the Internet can visit newsgroups at any time and read any articles of interest, whereas a mailing list delivers all messages posted directly to the subscribers' e-mail.

Types of Mailing Lists

Mailing lists can be one of several types, each with varying degrees of control. Following is a discussion of the major types of lists.

Moderated Lists

This type of list is maintained by a "gatekeeper" who filters out unwanted or inappropriate messages. If you try to post an advertisement where they are not permitted, your message will never make it out to the list of subscribers.

Unmoderated Lists

An unmoderated list is operated without any centralized control or censorship. Most lists are of this type. All messages are automatically forwarded to subscribers.

Digests

This is a compilation of many individual messages sent to each subscriber as one bulk message. Many digests contain a table of contents. The good thing about a digest is you do not receive as many separate e-mails and your mailbox doesn't become clogged up.

Targeting Appropriate Mailing Lists

There are thousands of publicly available lists online. There are a number of sites that provide lists of mailing lists. Three of the most popular and comprehensive are:

- The Liszt at *http://www.liszt.com*
- The List of Publicly Accessible Mailing Lists at *http://www.neosoft.com/internet/paml*
- Tile.net at *http://tile.net/lists*

Bulk E-mail
Group of identical messages e-mailed to a large number of addresses at once.

Spam
Sending the same message to a large number of people who didn't ask for it... sending people annoying mail

There are also companies online that specialize in providing targeted lists. One such company is Post Master Direct Response at *www.postmasterdirect.com*. This Company rents e-mail lists of people who have requested information on a particular topic.

Another option is to develop your own mailing list. This concept will be discussed later in this chapter.

Still another option is to purchase **bulk e-mail** lists. This is a questionable practice because it involves **spam**. Bulk e-mail lists are generally sold without the permission of the addressees, much like junk mailing lists. The recipients did not ask to be put on a mailing list. They are not aware of the fact that they are on a list and often do not appreciate being sent unsolicited e-mail. Another drawback is that usually these lists are not targeted. By using bulk e-mail lists you run the risk of not reaching any of your target market. You also risk annoying that portion of the addressees that under other circumstances may have been interested in what you were trying to sell.

The correct choice depends on the market you are targeting. Some people use the shotgun approach to reach as many people as possible. We've all received those e-mails... "reach 5 million with our mailing list available for $29.95." After all, one of the major benefits of the Internet is reaching large numbers of people quickly. This approach may have some merit if you are selling a mass-market product.

However, the best approach is to choose a list whose subscribers fit your target market as closely as possible. For example, if you are selling Geographic Information Systems to municipalities, a shotgun approach is a waste of both your time and resources. By using bulk e-mail you raise the ire of thousands of recipients of your e-mail, destroy your corporate image, and potentially damage your professional credibility. In this case, a much smaller targeted list should be used to get a much higher quality response rate.

Finding the Right Mailing List

You want to find a mailing list whose members are your target market. You will have to do your homework here as there are thousands of mail lists to choose from.

Meta-index
A long list of specific subject Internet resources

There are various **meta-indexes** of publicly available mailing lists where you can search by title or by subject. Some of these sites provide detailed information on the mail lists, like their content and the commands used to subscribe. We have provided information on a number of these resources in the Internet Resources section at the end of this chapter.

Once you have identified mail lists that have your target market as members you will subscribe to that list. To confirm that the list is appropriate for your marketing purposes, lurk a while to monitor the discussion taking place. Once this has been confirmed, you can begin participating in the list by providing valuable content. If advertising is not allowed, abide by the rules.

Subscribing to Your Target Mailing Lists

Liszt, *title.net/lists,* and the Internet Publicly Available Mailing Lists are great resources and will not only provide you with a huge list of accessible mailing lists but also specific instructions for joining the particular lists you are interested in. Most lists are subscribed to by sending an e-mail to the given address with "subscribe" in the subject or the body of the message. There are variations on this theme so you must check the instructions for joining each specific mailing list. After you subscribe you generally will receive an e-mail response with the rules, FAQs, and instructions on how to use the list.

For the most part, all of the rules for posting to newsgroups apply to mailing lists as well. Read the rules carefully and abide by them. A lurking period should be considered before you post a message. This will help you observe what types of messages are posted and the commonly accepted practices for that particular group.

Composing Effective Messages

As discussed in the previous chapter, your e-mails must be carefully prepared before you post to a mailing list. Remember to make your subject line relevant, keep your messages short and to the point, and always include your sig.file. If you are unsure whether your posting is appropriate for the group, you can simply send a test message to the moderator asking for advice.

Unlike newsgroups, the members of mailing lists receive all the messages directly into their mailbox every day. Some people prefer to receive the postings in *digest form*, that is, all the messages for that day are compiled into one e-mail sent to the recipient at the end of the day. The digest provides, at the beginning of the e-mail, a listing of all the messages with the "from" and "subject" identified followed by the complete messages. Thus, the content of the "subject" is extremely important.

You must never repeat the same or similar messages to a mailing list as you might do in a newsgroup. Once a member of a mailing list has seen your posted message they will not appreciate seeing it again, whereas a newsgroup has different readers all the time and similar postings are acceptable if they are timed appropriately.

The following tips on mailing list postings will assist you in becoming a respected member of their online community:

- Make sure that your messages are "on the subject." List subscribers don't want to hear announcements unrelated to their topic.

- You should be a regular contributor to your list before making any commercial announcement. If your mailing list does not allow advertising (most do not) use your sig. file. Sig.files are generally accepted. (See Chapter 4 for advertising when advertising is not allowed.)

- Track and record your responses when you use a new mailing list. You should have a "call to action" in your posting, encouraging the readers to visit a specific page on your site or to send e-mail to an e-mail address designated solely for this purpose. Only by employing an appropriate mechanism to track responses will you know with any certainty which mailing lists are successful and which are not.

- Set reasonable and achievable goals. As a benchmark, in most e-mail marketing campaigns a one percent to three percent response rate is considered a good response. However, if your mailing list is very targeted, and you are offering something of interest or value to a particular group, your response rates should be significantly higher.

Building Your Own Private Mailing Lists

You may want to build your own mailing lists. Generating your own mailing lists is often beneficial because of the many marketing uses the lists have. They can be used to maintain an ongoing dialog with existing customers regarding updates, support, specials, etc. They can also be used to communicate with current and prospective customers through distribution of corporate newsletters, price lists, new catalogues, product updates, new product announcements, and upcoming events.

You can use a number of methods for soliciting and collecting e-mail addresses, including an online guestbook or other type of registration form to be filled out on your web site. You can also have a "subscribe here" button where visitors can sign up for the mailing list on your site. Another way to get people to register for your mailing list is by offering an informative newsletter for the target market. Others provide freebie incentives such as T-shirts, software, or games. If you sign up for the newsletter at Lobster Direct (*www.lobsterdirect.com*) your name will be put in the draw for live lobsters.

Encourage customers and potential customers to subscribe to your electronic newsletter through traditional marketing techniques including press releases, offline newsletters, advertising, letters, etc.

If you use hardcopy direct mail, you can design a response that "captures" the e-mail addresses through a fax-back, business reply card, 1-800 number or by asking respondants to go to your web site or e-mail you directly. You can also ask people to sign up for your mailing list through newsgroup and mailing list postings, signature files, and other advertising.

You can boost your response rate by guaranteeing that responders' e-mail addresses will be kept confidential and not sold to anyone else.

Don't ever add someone's name to your mailing list without his or her permission. People really resent receiving unsolicited mail even if you give them the option to unsubscribe.

Starting Your Own Publicly Available Mailing List

To create your Internet mailing list, first you must give it a name that reflects the discussion that will take place and is enticing for your target market. Draft a FAQ or charter containing information on what the list is all about. Develop guidelines for participation.

You will need to find a place to host your mail list. There are many ISPs that host mail lists or you can use one of the many online mailing list hosting services. For lists and links of hosting service providers check out Vivian Neou's site at *http://www.catalog.com/vivian/mailing-list-providers.html.*

You should create a web page for your list to provide information about the list as well as its charter and guidelines. You should provide an opportunity to subscribe from the web site as well. This will add credibility to your mailing list.

Once the list is up and running you will have to advertise it so that people will actually subscribe. You can promote your list by participating in newsgroups that relate to your mail list topic. Remember not to post blatant ads where advertising is not allowed. Contribute to the newsgroup with your postings and use a tag line in your signature file to promote your mail list. You can also trade e-mail sponsorships with other mailing lists for promotion purposes.

There are a number of places to appropriately announce your list. One recommendation is the Internet Scout's New List, which you can find at *http://scout.cs.wisc.edu/scout/new-list/index.html*

Net Happenings is another announcement resource for new Internet resources. Gleason Sackson, the moderator of this list, has a huge following. To subscribe to Net Happenings, send an e-mail to majordomo@is.internic.net with "subscribe net-happenings" in the message area.

Get your mail list linked from the many lists of lists on the Internet. We have provided some of these in the Internet Resources at the end of this chapter. And make your list worth reading by ensuring that you and others have valuable information on the topic to share.

Escape the Unsolicited Bulk E-mail Trend

Bulk e-mail is any group of identical messages sent to a large number of e-mail addresses at one time. In some cases bulk e-mail lists have been developed from opt-in lists and the names are continually filtered through all of the universal remove lists. These lists are often categorized by subject and provide an acceptable marketing vehicle.

However, there are many bulk e-mail lists that have been developed by unscrupulous means, and the people on the lists have no interest or desire to receive unsolicited e-mail. Unsolicited bulk e-mail is the single largest form of e-mail abuse we have seen to date.

Over the last couple of years, more and more businesses on the Internet focus on services and software products catering to the bulk e-mail market. Software products have been developed that collect e-mail addresses from Usenet newsgroups, online service members' directories and forums, bots that look for "mailto:" codes in HTML documents online, publicly available mailing list subscribers, or even your site's visitors. Service companies that collect e-mail addresses and perform bulk mailings abound today on the Internet. Be very careful when considering bulk e-mail for online marketing purposes.

Internet Resources for Chapter 6

Lists of Mail Lists

Search the List of Lists - Mailing Lists
http://www.catalog.com/vivian/interest-group-search.html
Search one of the largest directories of special interest group e-mail lists (also known as *listservs*) available on the Internet.

Liszt, the Mailing List Directory
http://www.liszt.com
A very big directory of mailing lists–over 85,000 to date. The Liszt has organized its lists into subject categories. The Liszt provides details on how to subscribe to each of the mail lists in its database and provides information on content as well.

List of Publicly Available Mailing Lists
http://www.neosoft.com/internet/paml
The List of Publicly Accessible Mailing Lists is posted on this site and once each month to the Usenet newsgroups news.lists.misc and news.answers. The Usenet version is the definitive copy—this web version is generated from the database and uploaded several days after the Usenet version is posted. They continually post to Usenet so that the PAML will be archived at rtfm.mit.edu.

Reference.com
http://www.reference.com/
Reference.com makes it easy to find, browse, search, and participate in more than 150,000 newsgroups, mailing lists, and web forums. Reference.com does not break their listings down by subject categories, but you can do a keyword search. Information is provided on content as well as on subscribe commands. Reference.com allows list owners to archive their content for free. A clipping service is also available from this site where you enter search criteria and Reference.com forwards incoming mailing list messages that match.

The List Exchange
http://www.listex.com/imark.html
The Internet's one-stop mailing list resource. It links to a number of list sites and sites with information on building your lists.

L-Soft's CataList
http://www.lsoft.com/lists/listref.html
CataList, the catalog of listserv lists! From this page, you can browse any of the 19,516 public listserv lists on the Internet, search for mailing lists of interest, and get information about listserv host sites. This information is generated automatically from Listserv's Lists database and is always up to date.

The Internet Mailing List Network
http://www.listsnet.com/
ListsNet comprises a directory of publicly available mailing lists with browse and search capabilities. The mailing lists are categorized by subject and sub-topics.

Internet Marketing Mailing List
http://www.o-a.com
The Online Advertising Discussion List focuses on professional discussion of online advertising strategies, results, studies, tools, and media coverage. The list also welcomes discussion on the related topics of online promotion and public relations. The list encourages sharing of practical expertise and experiences between those who buy, sell, research, and develop tools for online advertising, as well as those providing online public relations and publicity services. The list also serves as a resource to members of the press who are writing about the subject of online advertising and promotion.

Usenet Newsgroup
news.lists
Gives you the list of new Usenet Newsgroups up and coming as well as the most popular ones.

AOL, Prodigy, and CompuServe
All have their own areas where you can search for mailing lists.

HTMARCOM
A mailing list that discusses high-tech marketing. To subscribe send the message "subscribe htmarcom your name" to the e-mail address *listserv@usa.net*.

Inside Connections
http://www.insideconnections.com
Offers business access to an e-mail list of consumers that want to receive e-mail announcements for particular types of products and services.

E-mail List Builder Programs

The Direct E-mail List Source
http://www.copywriter.com/lists/index.htm
Thousands of e-mail lists where you can advertise without spamming.

Avalanche 98
http://www.futuregate.com/avalanche/avalan.htm
Avalanche 98 provides small businesses with the power to send millions of newsletters, form mail, advertisements, and brochures with the click of a button using standard Internet connectivity.

Email Marketing 98
http://www.compwareusa.com/em98.html
Email Marketing 98 is a new high-end bulk e-mail marketing tool. At the push of a button, Email Marketing 98 will retrieve bulk e-mail addresses of the posters on an Internet news group or a series of groups. Then it will send your e-mail message to any or all of those addresses.

Extractor Pro
http://www.coolsoft.net/apps/extpro/enter.htm
Extractor 98 professes to be the best selling bulk e-mail software to date. Email Address Locator captures thousands upon thousands of targeted e-mail addresses in a matter of minutes. With Website Caller ID, you can find out who is visiting your web site and gather their e-mail address instantly. With Web Weasel, get targeted, free addresses from web pages automatically.

MaxdB Enterprises
http://www.maxdb.com/software/index.html
All kinds of e-mail software for the online marketer. DirectMail, NetContact, Stealth, Mach10, WebCollector, Sonic, GeoList, BulkMate, Desktop Server 98, Email Marketing 98, On Target 98, Atomic Harvester 98, and more.

Elmed Targeted Email Software
http://www.yug.com/tools/itools.htm
Information on, and links to, many e-mail marketing tools and software programs.

Web Wizard
http://www.yug.com/tools/webwiz.htm
Web Wizard is a 3-in-1 targeted e-mail address extraction program. It will retrieve e-mail addresses by keywords from Internet search engines and any web site or more than 50,000 newsgroups. Web Wizard will generate a targeted mailing list whenever you need one. Free downloadable demo. Software sells for $199.95.

Web Crumbs
http://www.thinweb.com
Web Crumbs gathers the e-mail addresses of visitors to your web site. This intelligent program can also manipulate what the visitor sees based on rules. Downloadable demo available from this site.

LISTBOT
http://www.listbot.com/
ListBot makes starting your own free e-mail list quick and easy. Use a ListBot e-mail list to stay in touch with friends and family, notify customers of new products and specials, find out who is visiting your web site and send updates, let your clubs, teams, classes, etc., talk by e-mail, create a forum for discussing favorite topic, publish an electronic newsletter, or connect any group of people by e-mail.

7

Grand Opening Tips for Your Web Site Virtual Launch

Just as you would have a book or software launch you can have a web site launch. In preparation for the web site launch you must develop an appropriate launch strategy. In this chapter we cover:

- Development of your web site launch strategy
- Web site announcement mailing lists
- Direct e-mail postcards to your customers or prospective clients

Cyberspace Virtual location where websites live

Launching and Announcing Your Web Site

A new web site or your new location in **cyberspace** can be launched in many of the same ways as you would launch a new physical store location. This may involve both online and offline activities. Just as you would prepare a book launch strategy or a new software product launch strategy you, can develop an appropriate *launch strategy* for your new web site.

Your Web Site Virtual Launch

A traditional store opening is accompanied by media attention. There are often invited guests, opening ceremonies, and gift giveaways. A web site virtual location launch occurs in cyberspace and the effectiveness of your launch can be increased with the following tips.

- Media attention can be generated through the distribution of press releases online and offline. (See Chapter 14 for press release distribution information.)
- Guests can be invited to your online opening through postings in newsgroups, newsletters, *What's New* sites, banner advertising, direct e-mail, signature files, as well as offline direct mail and advertising.
- Opening ceremonies can be just as exciting online as offline.
- You can feature special guests in chat areas for your grand opening.
- You can have contests that require visitors to visit various parts of your site to compete for prizes.
- You can have audio and video greetings from your site.
- You can have press releases regarding your opening available for download by the media.
- There is any number of other innovative "grand opening" attention grabbers that can be brainstormed with appropriate marketing and public relations individuals.
- Special free gifts can be provided to the first 20 or 50 visitors to your site.
- Do some offline advertising for your new URL (see Chapter 17 for innovative offline opportunities). or take advantage of online advertising via Announcement Sites (see Chapter 2 for information on announcing your site).

Internet Resources for Chapter 7

Netscape What's New
http://*netscape.com/home/whats-new.html*
This site selectively publishes information on new sites. To warrant a mention your site must somehow be unique...perhaps using the latest Netscape technologies.

Best-Web-Sites Announcement List
You can join this mailing list by sending the message "sub BESTWEB your name" to: listserv@vm3090.ege.edu.tr

Site Launch
http://www.sitelaunch.net
Site Launch offers guides, tools, and information for webmasters. Takes you through everything you need to get more visitors.

Nerd World What's New
http://www.nerdworld.com/whatsnew.html
The newest links added to Nerd World and a place to show off your site. Not just for nerds.

LaunchBot
http://www.launchbot.com
A listing of what's new on the home page front. Instructions here on how to get your site listed with them.

8

Develop a Dynamite Links Strategy

The more appropriate links you have to your site, the better! Expand your horizon by orchestrating links from related web pages to increase your traffic. In this chapter we cover:

- Developing a link strategy
- How to arrange links
- Get noticed—provide an icon and tag line hypertext for links to your site
- Link positioning
- Tools to check your competitors' links
- Using links to enhance your image

- Webrings
- Getting links to your site
- Reciprocal link pages

Everything Links to You

Link
A selectable connection from one word, picture, or information object to another

The more **links** you have to your site, the better chance you have that someone will be enticed to visit. However, the *quid quo pro* usually applies and this means providing reciprocal links, giving people the opportunity to leave your site with the click of a button. In order to minimize this "flight effect" place outbound links two or three layers down in your site to ensure visitors see everything you want them to see before they link out.

Regularly test all of the links from your site to ensure they are "live" and going to the appropriate locations. Dead links reflect poorly on your site.

Strategies for Finding Appropriate Link Sites

Ideally you should be linked from every high-traffic site that is of interest to your target market. You have to develop a strategy to find all of these sites and arrange links.

The first place to start is with the popular search engines. Most people use search engines and directories to find subjects of interest on the Internet. Most of the people searching never go beyond the first 20 to 30 results the search engine returns. Thus, these top 20 to 30 sites returned by the search engines must get a lot of traffic. Make sure you search relevant keywords in all the popular search engines and directories and investigate these top sites for appropriate link sites. Some of these sites will be competitors and may not want to reciprocate links. The best opportunity for links is with non-competing sites that have the same target market.

Another way to find appropriate link sites is to see where the leaders in your industry and your competitors are linked. See what your competition is doing. Determine where they are linked from, and decide whether these are sites that you should also be linked from. Learn what they are doing well, and also learn from their mistakes. You should be linked everywhere your competition is appropriately linked and them some.

Explore These URLs

There are many tools on the Internet to help you identify a web site's links. This is a great way to research where your site could be linked from, but isn't—yet!

These tools have been developed to assist you in finding who is linking to your site. In most cases you enter your URL, and then these tools provide you with the list of sites linking to your URL. However, these tools can be used just as easily to determine which sites are linking to your competition and industry leaders by entering *their* URL instead of your own. With the proper tools, you can obtain a list of locations on the Internet that are linked to these sites. These tools include Web Site Garage (Figure 8.1) , Alta Vista, Hot Bot, WebCrawler, Infoseek, Excite, and other search engines. Each of these will be discussed in more depth in the Resources section at the end of this chapter.

Visit each and every link to determine whether the site is one that is appropriate for you to be linked from. You should be able to pare down your list after identifying those sites that are inappropriate. Now you have a starting list of sites you want to link from.

Winning Approval for Potential Links

Now that you have a list of web sites you would like to be linked from, the next step is to identify the appropriate company contact from whom to request the link. Usually this can be found on the site.

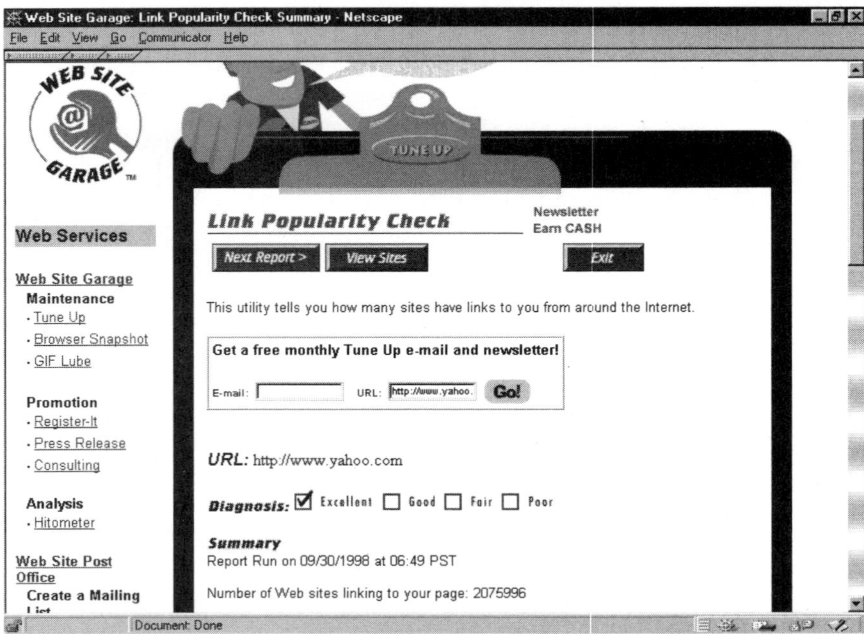

Figure 8.1. Web Site Garage provides many valuable tools. Their Link Popularity Check can be used to find who has linked to you from around the Internet. It can also provide valuable information on where your competitors are linked.

Titles such as Webmaster@ or any variation on the theme are usually a pretty safe bet. If the site does not have an appropriate contact, then try *feedback@*. You can either send the request there or ask for the e-mail address of the appropriate person.

Generally, a short note with the appropriate information in the subject line is most suitable. Your note should be courteous, briefly describe your site's content, and provide the rationale for why you think reciprocating links would result in a win-win situation. It doesn't hurt to compliment some aspect of the site that you think is particularly engaging.

It is a good idea to develop a generic "link request" letter that you can have on hand when you are surfing. When you find a site that is appealing from a link perspective, you can simply copy and paste the link request into an e-mail, do a little editing, and customizing, and hit the send button.

Here is an example of a link request e-mail.

Dear Web Site Owner,

I have just finished viewing your site and found it quite enjoyable. I found the content to be very valuable, particularly (customize here). My site visitors would appreciate your content as I think we appeal to the same demographic. My site, http://www.mysitename. com, focuses on (my site content) and would likely be of value to your visitors. If you have no objection, I would like to add a link to your site.

Sincerely,

John

When you get a response it will usually say that they would appreciate the link to their site and will offer to provide a reciprocal link. To facilitate this you should either have the HTML for the link ready to send or have it available on your site, or both.

By getting a referring link you are also helping your search engine rankings. Some of the search engines include the number of links to your site as part of their ranking criterion.

Make sure to follow up. If you said you would provide a reciprocal link, do so within 24 hours. Also make sure that you have been linked, ensure that the link works properly, and then remember to send a thank you.

Another way to get links is to *ask for them* on your site. In a prominent location on your site, place a link that says something like, "Would you like to provide a link to this site?" Link this message to your icon and HTML, with your tag line, and the hypertext link to your site.

You might want to consider offering an *incentive* to people who will provide you with a link. It could be something that

HTML (Hyper-Text Markup Language) The coding language that tells a web browser how to display a web page's words and images

can be downloaded or a free sample of your product in exchange for a link. This also provides you with another opportunity to market your site since you are giving something away for free, and thus you can be listed on the many Internet sites that identify sites for freebies.

Webrings
Interlinked web sites

Webrings are another source for links. For a complete discussion of webrings, see Chapter 16.

You may need to prompt sites to provide promised links. If you have made an arrangement for a link and, on follow up, find that the link is not there, it is appropriate to send an e-mail reminder. When sending the follow-up e-mail, include your icon, HTML, URL, and any other information that may be helpful.

Making Your Link the Place to 'Click'

There are links and then there are *links*. Usually links are your company name hypertext-linked to your home page, and your company's site link is listed with a number of other companies' links. Sometimes, if you are lucky, there is a brief description attached to the link.

You should take a proactive approach with linking arrangements. Explore every opportunity to have your link placed prominently and, if possible, to have it *differentiated* from the other links on the page.

Icon
An image that represents an application, a capability, or some other concept

Once you have an agreement with a site willing to provide a link, you should ask if you could send them an **icon** and the HTML for the link. The icon (.gif or .jpg format) should be visually pleasing and representative of your company. Within the HTML, include a tag line that entices people to click on the link. With the icon or logo, the tag line, and your company's name, your link will stand out from the rest. This is an example of what it should look like:

```
<IMG SRC="your gif/tif/bmp name"><A

HREF="http://www.yourdomainname.com">Catchy tag line

here</A></LI>
```

To Add or Not to Add with Free-for-All Links

There are thousands of free-for-all links on the Net. These sites allow you to add your URL to a long list of links. These sites provide little in the way of traffic unless you can have your link stand out from the rest.

One advantage you can get from being linked from these sites is in search engine ranking. As mentioned previously, some search engines use the number of links to your site in their ranking criterion.

Maintaining a Marketing Log

Record all new links to your site in your Internet marketing log. It is important to maintain this log and review it on a regular basis. You must periodically check to make certain that links to your site are operational and going to the appropriate location.

A Word of Caution with Link Trading

You must be aware when trading links that all links are not created equal.

- If you provide a prominent link to another site, make sure you receive a link of equal or greater prominence.
- Be aware, when trading your links with sites that receive substantially less traffic than you do, that you will probably have more people "link out" than "link in" from this trade.
- Don't ever put your outbound links directly on your home page. Have your outbound links located several levels down so visitors to your site will likely have visited all the pages you want them to visit before they link out from your site.

Internet Resources for Chapter 8

Tools to Find Who is Linking to Your Site

Web Site Garage
http://www.websitegarage.com.
This site has a link popularity summary that tells you from where and from how many a URL is linked.

Alta Vista
http://www.altavista.com
To find out where your competitors are linked using Alta Vista simply enter the competitor's URL in the search area like this: link:everyopportunity.com. This will return all pages in Alta Vista with a link containing the text everyopportunity.com.

Hot Bot
http://www.hotbot.com
Enter your competitor's URL in the search box and change the default from "all the words" to "links to this URL." When you type in the URL remember to include *http://*

WebCrawler
http://www.webcrawler.com/WebCrawler/Links.html.
Enter your competitor's URLs to find out how many links are provided to that page. WebCrawler provides the names of all the referring sites.

Infoseek
http://www.infoseek.com
Go to the Infoseek home page, and click on the Advanced Search link. Select WEB Advanced Search. Under "search the web for pages in which the:" choose hyperlink in the first drop-down menu. Select "must" in the second-drop down menu and "phrase" in the third drop-down menu. Then key in the URL you want to find in the space provided. Click on Search, and the results will show listings, with descriptions, of the sites that provide a link to your selected URL.

Excite and other search engines:
Just enter your competitors' URLs and see what comes up.

Reciprocal Link Exchanges

Missing Link - The Reciprocal Links Database
http://www.igoldrush.com/missing/
This database lets you search for like-minded sites you can contact for a mutually beneficial exchange of links.

Reciprocal Link Information

Virtual Promote
http://www.virtualpromote.com/guest6.html
This tutorial covers how to promote traffic to your web site with reciprocal links. This is a free service for all web site developers who want to learn more about announcing their web site and promoting more traffic to the Internet.

Free-for-All Link Pages For Your Site

Link Artist
http://linkartist.com/
Link Artist builds and hosts a free-for-all-page, just for your web site, and it costs you absolutely nothing. As a Link Artist member (remember, it's free), you will be able to place your banner ad in rotation throughout all the free-for-all pages they host.

Free-for-All Link Sites

Mega Linkage List
http://www.netmegs.com/linkage/
An exhaustive listing of over 1,500 directories, classified ad sites, little-known search engines, FFA pages, and more...all compiled for you alphabetically. Although there are some dead/broken links here,

a large majority are active, and you will be hard-pressed to visit each one.

Entrepreneurial Trend
http://www.angelfire.com/ct/suremoney/page2.html
Links to hundreds of places to list your site! Free-for-all link pages and search engines. Free classifieds and message boards. Free newsletters and reciprocal links.

Auto Link/Master Link
http://www.career-pro.com/autolink/index.cgi?autolink
AutoLink allows you to type in your site's URL, and with one click automatically list it on over 350 FFA pages, directories, and search engines. MasterLink is a brand new tool, and you must see it to truly appreciate this new concept in web site promotion. Highly recommended.

Link-O-Matic
http://www.linkomatic.com/index.cgi?10000
It allows you to submit your URL to 450+ quality promotional sites with one click, driving traffic to your web site and saving you loads of time.

9

Winning Awards/Cool Sites and More

There are literally hundreds of Cool Sites, Sites of the Day, Hot Sites, and Pick of the Week Sites. Some of these sites require you to submit while others are selected based on things like:

- Awesome graphics
- Dynamite content that is useful and interesting
- Uniqueness
- Fun features

If you are selected for one of these sites it can mean a huge increase in the number of hits to your site. You must be prepared for the increased traffic flow as well as the increased demand for online offerings. In this chapter we cover:

- Where to submit your site for award consideration
- How to win Site of the Day—tips, tools, and techniques

- Getting listed in What's New
- Posting your awards on your site
- Hosting your own Site of the Day

It's an Honor Just to be Nominated

There are sites that find and evaluate other sites on the Internet and recognize those that are outstanding by giving them an award. The award sites are generally very discriminating in terms of which sites are selected to be the recipients of their award. They have established criteria defining what is considered "hot" or "cool" and base their award selection on those criteria.

What's New web sites are designed to inform Internet users of new sites and updates to existing sites, and are often selective in which new sites they will promote. The owner of each site also selectively chooses awards for Site of the Day, Week, Month, and Year.

As discussed above, some of these sites require you to submit an announcement or site description and the awards are granted based on criteria such as graphics, dynamic content, uniqueness, and the "fun" quality of your site.

Other sites grant their awards based solely on the personal likes and dislikes of the owner of the site and do not adhere to any criteria at all.

Some awards are taken just as seriously as the Academy Awards. The Webby Awards, shown in Figure 9.1, have a very comprehensive nomination procedure. The following information regarding their process is available on their web site:

How to Win a Webby—Web Site Nomination Procedure

The International Academy of Digital Arts and Sciences (IADAS) is responsible for nominating and awarding each year's Webby Award and People's Voice Award winners. The 1998 awards were given out in 19 different content categories, including: Arts, Community, Education, Film, Games, Health, Home, Living, Money/Business, Music, News, Politics/Law, Print/Zines, Radio, Science, Sports, Travel, TV,

Figure 9.1. The Webbie Award.

and Weird. The site plans to expand the number of categories for The 1999 Webby Awards; possible new categories include Fashion, Humor, Homepages, and Youth. Nominees are selected by the International Academy of Digital Arts and Sciences' nominating committee for each category. Comprised of five journalists, experts, critics, scholars, or new-media professionals, the committee for each category collaborates to select five Webby Award nominees. The Academy does not accept any open submissions or outside suggestions.

When you win an award you post the award on your site for all to see. The award icon is usually a link back to the site that bestowed the honor on you.

Choosing Your Awards and Submitting to Win

There are different levels of prestige associated with each of the different award sites. Some are an honor to receive, such as a Starting Point Hot Site award. These awards are highly competitive because of the number of submissions they receive.

Other awards are easier to receive, such as those from commercial sites that give out awards in an attempt to increase the traffic to their own site. This results in traffic increases because the award is a graphic link displayed on the winner's site that visitors can follow back to the award giver's site. Other web masters give out awards to anybody and everybody who makes a submission. The award is granted with the sole purpose of building traffic.

The bottom line is that awards are valuable assets. The average web user cannot tell which awards are the prestigious ones and which are given to anyone that submits. So, submit for any awards that you

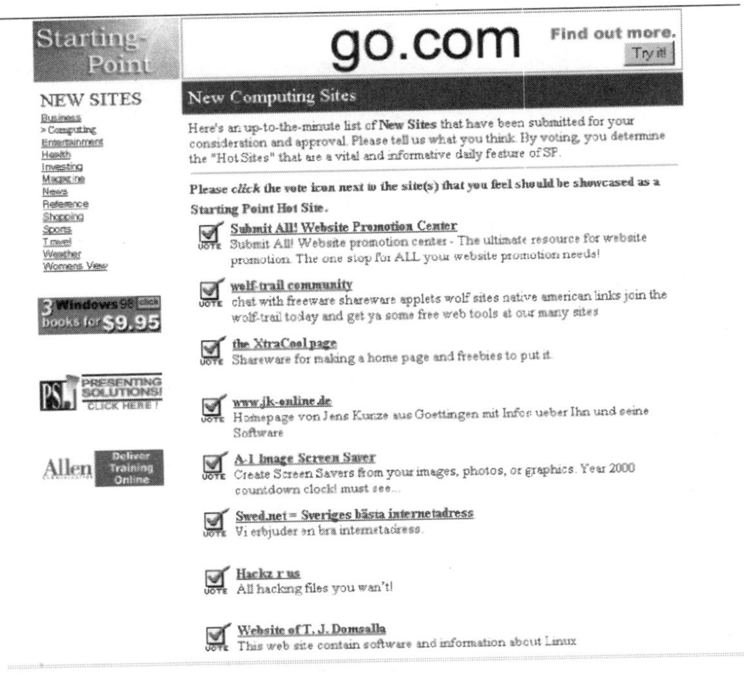

Figure 9.2. Starting Point's Hot Site Awards are very competitive.

choose to, as long as your site is *ready*. (A sample submission form is shown in Figure 9.3.)

Another item to determine before you submit for an award is whether the huge amount of new traffic will benefit your site. If you sell T-shirts emblazoned with WWW cartoons, then any traffic is good traffic, and awards will benefit your site. If on the other hand, you are a marine biologist specializing in red tides in the Arctic, then the traffic that "Site of the Day" would bring may be more of a hindrance than a help in marketing your services. Always determine if the marketing tools and techniques will increase hits from your target market before deciding whether to include them in your online marketing strategy.

Getting mentioned on one of the Cool Sites lists is probably the single biggest way to draw traffic to your site. Cool Sites does not just list anybody, and the traffic they send to your site is like a flash flood

What's New sites accept submissions for sites that they review. The best of the best are then placed prominently on their home page for all to see. It is considered to be quite an honor to develop or own

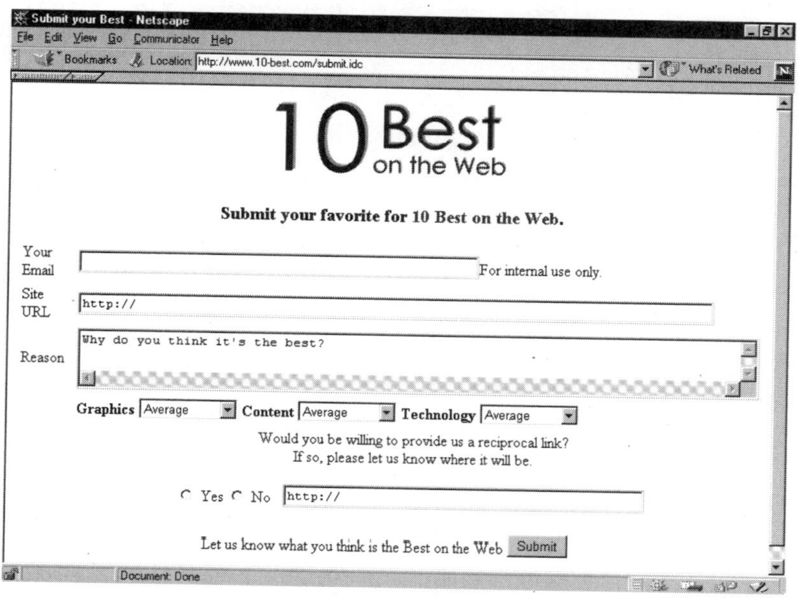

Figure 9.3. Sample award submission form. This one is for the 10 Best of the Web Award.

a site that has been selected by some of the more discriminating What's New sites.

The traffic will be swift and plentiful after you win one of these awards. Be prepared! Have a plan that you can implement on a moment's notice. If you offer something free from your site, ensure you can access a huge volume of whatever it is and ensure you have a plan to distribute quickly. If you offer a free download from your site, plan to have a number of alternate **FTP** sites available to your visitors. If you have a "call in" offer, ensure you have a telephone response system in place and staff to handle the huge volume of calls you may get. You will need a plan to handle the huge volume of e-mails you will get as well.

FTP (File Transfer Protocol) The simplest way to exchange files between computers on the Internet

Once you have decided that the type of traffic that comes along with winning the award fits with your marketing strategy, you should make sure your site has the makings of a winner and then submit to as many award sites as you can.

- First, make a list of the URLs of these award sites.
- Understand the submission form and guidelines. Review a number of forms to determine the common information requested.
- Develop a document with the answers to the various questions from which you can copy and paste into the different submission forms (this will save you time).
- Submission forms will capture the following types of information:
    - URL
    - Title of your site
    - Contact person (name, e-mail, phone, address)
    - Owner of the site
- Submission guidelines will tell you what type of sites can be submitted; i.e. some awards do not accept personal pages while

others do not include commercial sites. The submission guidelines will also tell you what meets their definition of "Cool" or "New" and what doesn't.

- Some award sites require that you display their award icon on your site. Posting an award on your site can provide a number of positive results—including enhanced credibility.

What's Hot and What's Not in the Name of Cool

Most of the award sites will provide you with their selection criterion. Some award sites look for and base their selection on valuable content while other award sites look for innovative and unique capabilities. While sites vary on what they consider "Hot" or "Cool,"they are fairly consistent on what doesn't make the grade, as summarized below.

What's Hot
- Awesome graphics
- Great, original content
- Broad appeal
- Fun feature

What's Not
- Single page sites
- Single product promotion
- Offensive language or graphics
- Lengthy download time

Becoming the Host of Your Own Awards Gala

You can also create your own award program in order to draw traffic to your site; however, this requires a huge amount of work to maintain. You will need to work at it on a daily or weekly basis so you must be committed to it. Be sure there is a benefit from a marketing perspective before you design and develop your own award program. You must also be prepared to conduct your own searches at the outset to find sites to promote if the quality of sites being submitted to you is poor.

- You will first have to develop the criteria you will use in your site selection.

- You will have to develop several web pages related to the award (information on selection criteria, submission forms, today's or this week's award winner, past award recipients page, etc.) in order to promote the award. (Ensure that you stipulate that you are looking for submissions from commercial sites or personal pages and what type of criteria will be used in judging the submissions.)

- You will have to have your award icon developed. Have this icon link back to your site. The award distinguishes the winner, thus the link will probably be displayed prominently on the their site. This is a great traffic builder.

- Finally, you have to announce the award and market, market, market.

Internet Resources for Chapter 9

Awards

Lycos Top 5%
http://point.lycos.com/categories/index.html
Your personal guide to the best sites on the web. The Top 5% is a selective directory of top-shelf sites rated by the web's most experienced reviewers.

Webby Awards
http://www.webbyawards.com
The Webby Awards have been embraced by the online community as the leading creative honors for digital media. The awards recognize the most creative and innovative web sites of the year and the talented editorial, technical, and design teams behind them.

Best of the Planet Awards
http://www.2ask.com
Called the people's choice award where you can decide who's best.

Best of the Web Awards
http://botw.org/
This award aims to highlight those places that best show the quality, versatility, and power of the World Wide Web.

PC Magazine's Top 100 Web Sites
http://www.zdnet.com/pcmag/special/web100/index.html
A list of top sites listed in five categories, everything from amazing online stores to essential computing resources, with a couple of stops along the way for fun and entertainment.

Platinum 100
http://www.firestorm.com/plat98.html
Featuring the Best of the Web, this is their fourth year selecting the best sites on the net. This site reviews and awards the Top 100 Sites on the net in different categories.

High Five Award
http://www.highfive.com
Each week they review well-designed web sites and discuss how to make your site become a killer.

What's New

Netscape's What's New
http://home.netscape.com/netcenter/new.html?cp'hom09snew
Netscape is selective in their What's New section, they don't just list every site. Selection is generally based on great sites that use advanced Netscape features.

Yahoo!
http://www.yahoo.com/new
Yahoo!'s "what's new" on the web.

What's New Too
http://newtoo.manifest.com
New announcements are posted to this site within 36 hours of submission, and the list, which is lengthy, is updated daily.

NCSA Mosaic What's New Page
http://www.ncsa.uiuc.edu/SDG/Software/Mosaic/Docs/whats-new.html
The NCSA What's New receives thousands of submissions each week. It takes several weeks to appear after submission and the page is updated daily. Sites appear alphabetically.

Whatsnew.com
http:www.whatsnew.com
This is a seven-days-a-week, continuously updated, fully searchable directory of new Internet web sites.

Hot Sites/Cool Sites

USA Today Hot sites
http://www.usatoday.com/life/cyber/ch.htm
USA Today scours the web for sites that are hot, new, and notable. Visit their daily list to find some of the best sites the web has to offer. They look for sites that may stretch the design envelope and show where the web is headed...sites that offer something unusual or unexpected, or something just plain useful.

Starting Point Hot Site
http://www.starting-point.com
Votes are taken from their What's New section for sites worthy of a Hot Site Award.

100 Hot Web sites
http://www.100hot.com/
Directory of web sites based on web traffic and organized by category.

Cool Site of the Day
http://www.coolsiteoftheday.com
Cool Site of the Day is a wildly popular Internet award site that features interesting, provocative, and irreverent web sites from around the world.

Mush Net Hot Site Award
http://www.mush.net/hotsite.html

This award is presented by a panel of lay persons to sites which in the panel's opinion merit special mention, outstanding content, and valuable service provided to the Internet community.

Cool Central Site of the Hour
http://www.coolcentral.com
Delivers the best new web sites the moment they are discovered. Featuring Cool Central Site of the Moment, Hour, and Nick Click, Private...Eye.

Netscape What's Cool
http://home.netscape.com/netcenter/cool.html
Netscape's picks of the coolest web sites.

Virtual Reference Meta-Index of Award Sites
http://www.refdesk.com//textcool.html
A listing of different sites that host site of the day, hot sites, etc.

Cool Banana Site of the Day
http://www.coolbanana.com
Cool Banana provides the best of the web daily! The site offers depth and content with great innovative design. Their "Webmonkeys" choose sites that don't require a T1, plug-ins, or any specific browser.

Tools

WPRC
http://www.wprc.com/fldb/dbase/hot/dbhot.html
A great site with links to submission forms for Hot Sites, Cool Sites, and Sites of the Day awards.

Free Links Award Sites
http://www.freelinks.com/awards.html
This is a free service to aid and simplify your web site promotion efforts. You can also find information on databases, search engines, and link pages where you can list your site for free.

10

Maximizing Promotion with Meta-Indexes

Meta-indexes are intended to be useful resources for people who have a specific interest in a particular topic. Meta-indexes are a large and valuable resource to reaching your target audience and should be utilized to their full potential. In this chapter we cover:

- What meta-indexes are
- Why meta-indexes are useful
- How to make the link to your site stand out
- How to create your own meta-index

What Are Meta-Indexes?

Meta-indexes are lists of Internet resources pertaining to a specific subject category and are intended as a resource for people who have a specific interest in that topic. These lists, like the one for Cybermalls shown in Figure 10.1, consist of a collection of URLs of related Internet resources and are arranged on a web page by their titles. The owners or creators of meta-indexes put a lot of effort into compiling these lists and are eager to find new sites to add to them. They will often list your site for free—since the more related sites they have, the more "meta" their index is. So if you come across a meta-index that is associated with the topic of your site, feel free to ask for a link.

Meta-indexes are directed at a specific topic, such as "pets" or "cars." Meta-indexes provide easy access to a number of sites on a specific topic, and they are a great way to draw targeted, interested people to your web site. In addition, some users may rely on meta-indexes as their only search effort. They may not use a search engine to perform a query on Mexican resorts, for example, if they know a certain meta-index contains 200 sites on Mexican resorts. Meta-in-

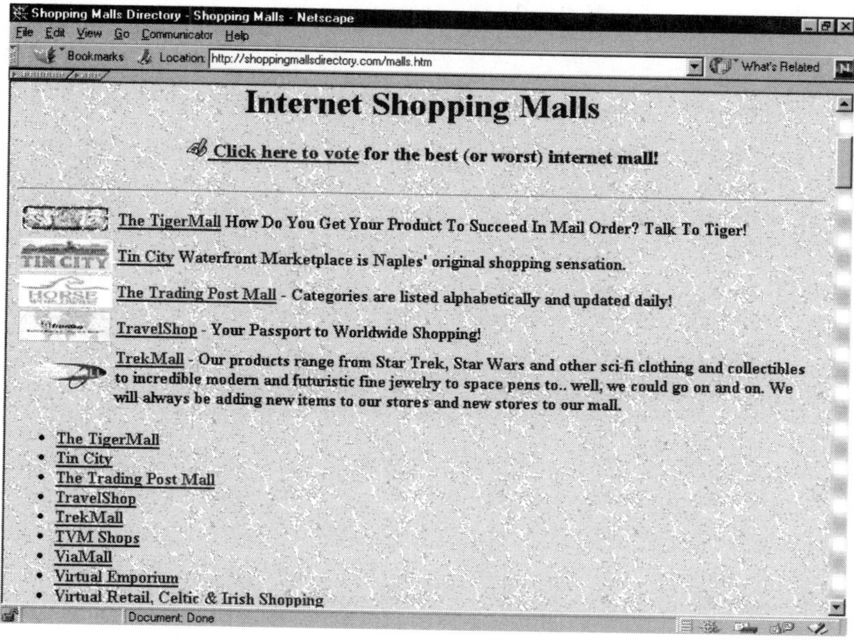

Figure 10.1. Internet shopping malls—a cybermall meta-index.

dexes can increase your chances of being found by people who are interested in what you have to offer.

Enlisting Meta-Indexes for Optimal Exposure

To ensure that you are taking full advantage of meta-indexes, do the following:

- Source appropriate meta-indexes
- Request a link
- Provide the details necessary
- Look at sponsorship or banner advertising opportunities

Meta-indexes can be arranged by subject (sites that provide information on book publishing) or by geography (tourist sites in Alaska). The major search engines are a good place to start. For example, to find tourist sites in Alaska, conduct a search on +Alaska+tourist+directory. Once you find a good list and start to check the links, you will likely find other lists through the first list. Bookmark or keep a record of the meta-indexes you like for future reference.

If you are not sure if your site will be accepted by a certain meta-index, send a request anyway. Meta-lists draw more traffic when they provide more resources to their readers, so list owners may be fairly lenient on what's acceptable and what's not.

When requesting a link to your site send an e-mail with "site addition request" in the subject area of your message. Include the following in the body of the message:

- URL
- Description of your site
- Explain why you feel your site is appropriate for the list

- Your contact information in your signature file (see Chapter 4)

Once you have identified indexes that appeal to your target market, determine whether additional opportunities might exist for sponsorship or purchasing banner advertising on the site. Meta-indexes that relate to your market are a great place to advertise since they are accessed by your target customer.

Keep in mind that the compilers of meta-indexes are motivated by non-commercial reasons and are under no obligation to add your site to their list or process your request quickly. However, because of the banner advertising revenue potential, there are more and more meta-index sites that have a commercial focus.

To make your link stand out among the many others listed, inquire about adding a prominent link or icon to the meta-index page along with a short tag line, in addition to your company name. If you provide the .gif and the HTML, the meta-index owner may be happy to include it.

Review the Work of Some Meta-Index Giants

- **Dentistry Meta Indices (see Figure 10.2):** *http://www.nus.sg/NUSinfo/DENT/indice.htm*
- **GIS Resources on the Web:** *http://www.gsd.harvard.edu/~pbcote/GIS/web_resources.html*
- **Bookmarks About Jazz:** *http://www.sainet.or.jp/~head/Jazz.html*
- **Education Related Web Sites K-12:** *http://teach.virginia.edu/curry/resources/library/edrelatedwebsites.html*
- **Australia Travel Directory:** *http://www.anzac.com/aust.htm*

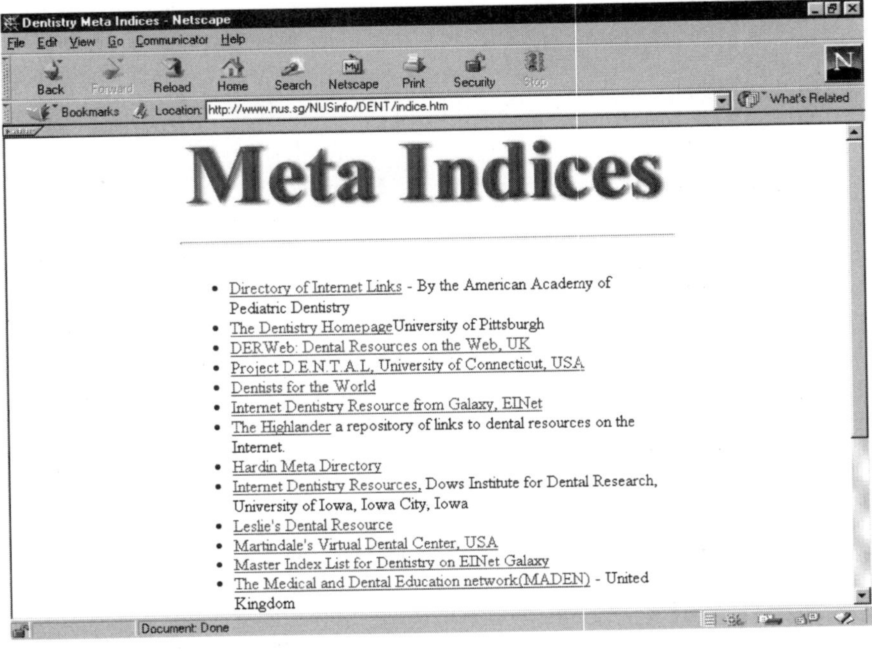

Figure 10.2. Meta-index for the dental industry.

- **Hotels and Travel on the Net:**
  http://www.hotelstravel.com/homepage.html

Internet Resources for Chapter 10

WWW Meta-indexes and Search Tools
http://www.fys.ruu.nl/~kruis/h3.html
A Library of Congress Internet Resource Page

Argus Clearinghouse
http://www.clearinghouse.net
The premier Internet research library (or meta-index) to locate everything you need to find on the web.

The Ultimate Directory - Infospace
http://www.infospace.com
InfoSpace calls itself the Ultimate Directory! You'll find yellow pages, white pages, classifieds, shopping sites, investing information, government listings, chat rooms, and much more.

Virtual Library
http://vlib.org/Overview.html
The Virtual Library is the oldest catalog of the web, started by Tim Berners-Lee, the creator of the web itself. Unlike commercial catalogs, it is run by a loose confederation of volunteers, who compile pages of key links for particular areas in which they are expert. Even though it isn't the biggest index of the web, the VL pages are widely recognized as being among the highest-quality guides to particular sections of the web.

Internet Basics Hotlink Internet Resources
http://www.key-concepts.com/hotlinks/Int-Bscs.htm
Meta-index of Internet demographics and statistics, how to search the web, Metasearch tools, people finding directories, more ways to locate people, "help" Internet user groups, e-mail resources, chat resources, personalized news services, and Usenet resources.

W.E.D. The World E-mail Directory
http://www.worldemail.com/
WED World E-mail Directory has estimated access to more than 18,000,000 e-mail addresses and more than 140,000,000 business and phone addresses worldwide. One of the fastest growing engines for people, businesses and organizations.

@LinkPad
http://www.referthem.com/pad/links.htm
A meta Index of Meta Indexes. This site has indexes ranging from advertising, e-zines, and e-mail to web graphics and real estate.

11

Productive Online Advertising

"Banner advertising works!" according to Forester Research. Advertising online provides visibility—just as offline advertising does. You must develop a banner advertising strategy that works with your product and your budget. In this chapter we cover:

- Your online advertising strategy
- Advertising opportunities on the web
- Banner ad design and impact on click-throughs
- Banner ad sizes and locations
- Placing classifieds
- Tips to creating dynamite banner ads that work
- The cost of advertising online
- Measuring ad effectiveness
- Banner ad exchange networks

- Using an online advertising agency
- Sources of net advertising information

Expanding your Exposure Through Internet Advertising

Today Internet advertising is being recognized in the advertising budgets of businesses and organizations around the globe. Banner ads are a way to create awareness of your web site and increase the traffic to it. Your web site is your online presence. Banners are placed on the sites that your target market is likely to frequent, thus encouraging this market to click-through and visit you!

The Internet offers many different advertising spaces. Banner ads can be placed on search engines, content sites, advertising sites, and online magazines. The choice of where your ad is displayed is based on the objectives you wish to achieve with your online advertising strategy.

There are a number of major advantages to online advertising:

- The response from these ads is easily measured within one day.
- The amount of information that can be delivered, if your web site is visited, far surpasses that of a traditional advertising campaign.
- The cost of maintaining an online advertising campaign is much less than using traditional media.

Maximize Advertising with Your Objectives in Mind

When developing your advertising strategy, you will need to determine the objectives of your advertising campaign. The most common objectives for an online advertising campaign include:

- Building brand awareness

- Increasing web site traffic
- Generating leads and sales

You have a number of choices to make, such as what type of advertising to use and where to advertise. These choices should be made based on your objectives. If it is your objective to increase the overall brand recognition, then a nicely designed banner ad on one of the high-traffic search engines would be effective. If you would like to develop leads and find new clients, then a more targeted approach should be taken.

When deciding how to proceed with your advertising strategy, consider how many people you want to reach. Do you want a high-quality response from a small number of very targeted people, or do you want to reach a massmarket audience of grand proportions?

Think about the people you are targeting. If you sell dentistry supplies to dental practices, then you want to target dentists and hygienists. It would not make much sense to put an ad on Yahoo! when you could advertise on a site about new medical discoveries in dentistry.

Always keep your budget in mind when you are devising your online advertising strategy. There are many ways to stretch your advertising dollar. If you have the time you can find appropriate sites to trade banners. You can also participate in banner exchange programs.

Online Advertising Terminology

Banner Ads

Banner ads are small advertisements that are placed on a web site. Companies usually develop their banner ads, find appropriate sites for placement, and then either purchase or trade banner space.

Click-Throughs

When a viewer clicks on a banner ad with their mouse and goes to the site advertised, it is called a "click-through." Sometimes banner advertising prices are determined by the number of click-throughs.

Hits

Hits to a site are the number of times that another computer has accessed that site (or a file in a site). This does not mean that if your site has 1,000 hits that 1,000 people have visited your site. If your home page has a number of graphic files on it, this number could be very misleading. A hit is counted when the home page main file is accessed, but a hit is also counted for every graphic file that loads along with the home page. So if a person visits 6 pages on a site and each page has 4 graphics there would be 30 hits generated.

Impression

When someone views a banner ad it is called an impression. Banner advertising prices are often calculated by impressions. If a person visits a page 6 times, this will generate 6 impressions.

CPM

Cost per thousand impressions or CPM is a standard advertising term. CPM is often used to calculate the cost of banner advertising. If the price of banner advertising on a site was $40 CPM, and the number of impressions the ad had was 2000, then the advertiser would have to pay $80 for displaying the ad.

Jump on the "Banner" Wagon

Banner advertising is the most common and most recognized form of online advertising. Banner ads are available in various sizes, as shown in Figure 11.1, but the most common banners are displayed at roughly

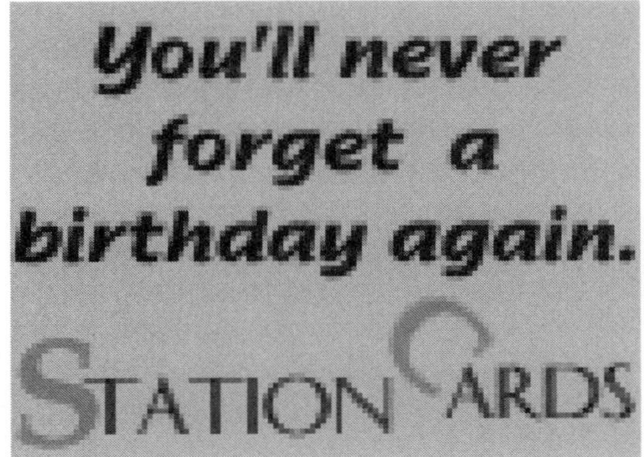

Figure 11.1. Banner ads come in all shapes and sizes.

468 x 60 pixels. Banners usually have an enticing message or call to action that coaxes the viewer to click on it. "What is on the other side?" you ask...the advertisers web site, of course. Banner ads can also be static, just displaying the advertiser's logo and slogan, or animated with graphics and movement.

The banner ad is designed to have a direct impact on the number of click-throughs it will achieve. There are a number of resources online to assist you in developing dynamic banner ads. The Banner Generator at *http://www.coder.com/creations/banner* allows you to create banners online at no charge. The Media Builder at *http://www.mediabuilder.com/abm.html* provides you the opportunity to develop animated banner ads directly from their site. Other resources to assist you in designing and building banner ads are identified in the Resources section at the end of this chapter.

There are a wide variety of banner sizes available. You should consult with the owners of the web sites on which you want to advertise *before* creating your banner ad or having one created professionally for you.

The objective of your banner ad is to have someone click on it. Do not try to include all of your information in your ad. A banner that is too small and cluttered is difficult to read and is not visually appealing. Many banners simply include a logo and a tag line enticing the user to click on it. Free offers or contest giveaways are also quite effective for click-throughs since they tend to appeal to the user's curiosity.

Exploring Your Banner Ad Options

Static banners are as the name suggests. They remain static on the same web page until they are removed. Your banner ad will be visible on that particular page until your reader moves to another page.

Rotating banners are banner ads that rotate among different web pages on the same site. Some rotating banners rotate every 15 or 30 seconds so a visitor may see several ads while remaining on the page. Other rotating banner ads rotate every time there is a new visitor to the page. Rotating banners are commonly used in high-traffic web sites.

Scrolling banners are similar to modern billboards. Here the visitor will see a number of billboard ads, scrolled to show a different advertisement every 10 to 30 seconds.

Follow the tips below to ensure that your banner ad will achieve your marketing objectives.

- Make sure that your banner ad is quick to load. If your web page loads in its entirety before the banner, then the viewer may click away before ever seeing it. The best banner ads load before the page does, permitting the viewer to read the banner at first sight. Keep your banner ad size under 10k.

- Keep it simple! If your banner contains too much text, (as seen in Figure 11.2) animation, too many colors and fonts, this will cause viewers to experience information overload. Viewers will not be encouraged to read or click on your banner.

- Make sure your banner ad is legible. Many banners on the Internet are nicely designed, but are difficult to read. Use an easy-to-read font with the appropriate size. Be careful in your choice of color.

- Make sure your banner ad links to the appropriate page in your site. It is not uncommon to click on an interesting banner only to find an error message waiting for you. This is very annoying to Internet users and counter-productive to your marketing effort.

- Check your banner ads on a regular basis to verify that the link remains active.

Figure 11.2. Banners that are too busy are counter-productive.

- Make your ads interesting. Don't simply say "click here." Give your audience a compelling reason to do so.
- If you know absolutely nothing about advertising and graphic design, do not try to create a banner on your own. Go to a professional. If you do design your own banner, get a second opinion.

Banner Ad Price Factors

The price of banner ad space varies from site to site. Banner ads are often sold based on the number of impressions or number of click-throughs. As stated earlier, an impression is an ad view, and click-throughs are the actual clicking on the banner. The price per impression should be less than the price per click-through. Banner ad pricing per CPM (cost per 1000 impressions) is between $10 and $90 depending on the site you are advertising on—how targeted the audience is, and how much traffic it receives. Search-engine banner ads range between $20 and $50 CPM. Keyword advertising ranges between $40 and $70 CPM. The click-through pricing is somewhere between $.20 and $1.20 per click-through, again depending on the site and the traffic. Before you sign anything, make sure that you understand what you are paying for.

When site owners charge per impression, there is usually a guarantee that your ad will be seen by a certain number of people. The burden is on the seller to generate traffic to their site. When the charges are per click-through, the responsibility is on you, the advertiser, to design an ad that will encourage visitors to click on it. Sites that charge per impression are more common than those that charge per click-through.

There are obvious advantages to the advertiser when paying per click-through. They don't have to pay a cent for the 10,000 people that saw their banner but did not pursue the link.

Another method used to determine banner ad pricing is by how targeted the audience is. A good example is the site *http://www.everyopportunity.com*. At this site, entrepreneurs research a database of over 4,000 franchise opportunities, distributorships, home-based business opportunities, and other information on business opportunities—hence the name *every opportunity.com*. This location would be more valuable to a franchisor than most other sites because of the highly specific target market...in this case, prospective franchisees!

For sites that do *not* have a large volume of traffic, a flat rate is often charged for a specified period of time.

Making it Easy with Online Advertising Agencies

If your objective is to reach a large number of users through a wide variety of sites, Internet advertising agencies may be appropriate. If you are not familiar with the process of buying and selling ad space, these resources can be particularly beneficial.You may have to pay a little more initially, but it could save you in the long run. See the Resources section at the end of this chapter for the names of some agencies.

Saving Money with Banner Exchange Programs

Banner exchanges work much as you would expect, i.e. your ad is placed on other sites in exchange for someone else's banner ad placed on your web site.

To register with a banner exchange you often have to go through a qualifying process. What this means is that your site has to meet certain minimum standards. Once you have passed the test, the banner exchange will provide you with HTML code to insert into pages of your site where the banner ads will appear. Every time this HTML is accessed, a random banner ad appears for the viewer to see.

This process is monitored and tracked. Each banner that is accessed from the exchange and displayed to a visitor earns you some sort of credit or token. These credits or tokens are used within the banner exchange like a bartering system. The credits you earn are exchanged for having your banner displayed on another site.

Sometimes some of the credits you earn go to the banner exchange itself, as a fee for managing the process. The banner exchange will sell the credits to paying advertisers or use them to promote the exchange. Some banner exchanges will allow you to focus your exposure on your target market.

When determining which banner exchanges to belong to, look for restrictions. When banner exchanges have no restrictions, you never know what could be loading to your pages. Don't join banner exchanges without size specifications for the banners. Your site could be displaying huge 150 x 600 pixel banners that make your visitors wait while they load. Ensure that the load time of every banner displayed on your site will be reasonable.

Here are some of the more popular online banner exchange programs. A more complete listing is available in the Resources section of this chapter.

- LinkExchange: *http://www.linkexchange.com*
- SWWWAP: *http://www.swwwap.com*
- Trade Banners: *http://ww.resourcemarketing.com/banner.htm*
- World Tech Media: *http://www.narrowcastmedia.com*

Bartering for Mutual Benefits with Banner Trading

Using this technique requires you to barter with other web sites to trade banners with their sites. If you are browsing the Internet and find a site that you think appeals to your target market, then ask for a trade. Send the webmaster an e-mail outlining your proposition. Include the reason why you think it would be mutually beneficial, a description of your site, where you would place their banner on your site, and where you think your banner might go on their site.

When you make arrangements like this, be sure to monitor the results. If the other site has low traffic, then more visitors may be leaving your site through their banner than are being attracted. Also, check the other site regularly to make sure that they are still displaying you banners for the duration agreed to.

Associate Programs

Along with the increase in banner advertising budgets of online companies, we are seeing more sites willing to offer services to capture their share. Associate programs have begun to spring up all over the Net. The premise of these programs is that a web master places a clickable banner ad on their site. If a visitor clicks-through and this results in a sale or a lead, a commission is paid to the banner hosting site. The fee can vary from a few cents to several hundred dollars. It can be based on a percentage or a flat fee per sale basis.

Location, Location, Location

As with all types of advertising, the location of the ad is extremely important. There are any number of places that you can place your banner ads online. Always ensure that your banner advertising location is consistent with your objectives.

Search Engines

If your goal is to reach as many different people as possible, high-traffic search engine sites are where you should be. Cost per thousand (CPM) impressions is usually $20-$50. If your target market is more selective, then a more targeted buy within the search engine is appropriate. Targeted buys can include tying your banner ad to specific keywords (i.e., every time the keyword is used in a search your banner ad would appear). Targeted ads generally range in price from $40-$90 CPM but are quite often worth the extra price because of the correlation to the targeted buyer.

Content Sites

If your objectives include bringing interested people from your target market to your site, then advertising on appropriate content sites would be extremely effective. These are sites that concentrate on a specific topic. The cost of advertising on content sites ranges from $25-$50 CPM depending on the traffic volume they see and the focus of their visitors.

Tips for Succeeding with Classified Ads

Classified ads are also displayed on the Internet on various web sites. Some sites offer to display classified ads for free, while others will charge a small fee.

Here are some great tips for creating effective classified ads:

- *Headlines.* The headline of your ad is very important. The subject line determines how many people will read the rest of your ad. Look at the subject lines of other ads and see what attracts your eye.

- *Entice.* Use your classified ad to get people to request more information, not to get immediate orders. You can then send them a personalized letter outlining all of the information and making a great pitch to attract an order.

- *Be Friendly.* Your classified shouldn't be formal and business like. Make your ad light and friendly.

- *Call for Action.* Do not only offer information about what you are selling. Call the reader for action; for instance, to order now!

- *Do Some Tests.* Run a number of different ads and use a different e-mail address for each one. This way you can determine which ad receives the most responses. You can then run the best ad in a number of different places to find out which place gets the biggest response.

- *Keep a Record.* Keep records of your responses so that you will know which ads were the most successful.

Form Lasting Advertising with Sponsorships

Sponsorships are another form of advertising that usually involves strong, long-lasting relationships between the sponsors and the owners of the sites. Sponsors may donate money and equipment to web site owners in this mutually beneficial relationship.

Commercial Links

Another form of online advertising is commercial links. There are a number of targeted sites that provide a lengthy list of URLs related to a specific topic. These sites will often charge a fee to have a link from their site to yours. There are also web sites where you can be listed if you don't have a web site and would prefer to only have your business name and phone number or e-mail address listed.

Sponsoring a Mailing List

Another online advertising opportunity is presented by mailing lists. Mailing lists provide a very targeted advertising vehicle. Mailing list subscribers are all interested in the list topic and are therefore potential clients, if you select the mailing list appropriately. The rates for sponsoring lists are quite low. The cost would be determined on a price-per-reader basis and is usually between 1 and 10 cents per reader. Subscribe to the lists that have appeal to your target market and read the FAQs to determine whether advertising or sponsorship opportunities exist for each mailing list. Refer to Chapter 6 for more information.

Online and Offline Promotion

Your advertising strategy shouldn't be limited to online activities. It is important to integrate your offline advertising strategy to include promotion of your web site. For more information on Offline Promotion see Chapter 17.

Internet Resources for Chapter 11

Banner Ad Tools

The Banner Generator
http://www.coder.com/creations/banner
The Banner Generator is a free service to let you create graphical banners for your web pages.

The Media Builder
http://www.mediabuilder.com/abm.html
Create your own custom animated banners right here. No fancy plug-ins or hard thinking required.

Online Banner Creator
http://www.crecon.com/banners.html
Create your own banner in minutes for free from this site.

Animated Communications
http://www.animation.com
Another online resource to build your own animated banners in minutes.

Creative Connectivity
http://www.crecon.com
Home of the Instant Online Banner Creator.

Online Advertising Agencies

MMG The Online Agency
http://www.mmgco.com/index.html

MMG specializes exclusively in online media planning, buying, tracking, and reporting. They combine state-of-the-art technology with expert knowledge to place advertising for clients in the right place, before the right audience, at the right time, and for the right price. For companies with quarterly online advertising budgets of $100,000 or more.

Thielen Online
http://www.thielenonline.com/index.htm
Full-service advertising agency, located in Fresno and Sacramento, California, with strategic online marketing and complete web site development capabilities.

Lunar Group Interactive
http://www.lunargrp.com/tips2.html
Lunar Group Interactive is a full-service advertising agency with expertise in traditional mediums, as well as one that embraces the future of marketing. Clients include Casio and Imtech.

@dVenture
http://adsonline.miningco.com/mlibrary.htm
@dVenture, the online division of Venture Direct Worldwide, is the solution for over 500 advertisers looking to drive traffic, generate leads, sales, branching, or advertising revenue. Fifteen years of direct marketing experience coupled with four years of online expertise assures some of the best marketing, sales, planning, research, targeting, buying, creative, and reporting available. @dVenture is a leading Internet advertising network providing advertisers with the opportunity to promote their company, products, and services to Internet users. With three buying options. @dVenture offers advertisers global reach as well as targeted Internet marketing.

Banner Exchanges

The Banner Exchange
http://www.bannerexchange.com
When you register you agree to show banners on your site. Each time a banner is displayed on your site you receive half a credit. For every full credit you accumulate, your banner will be shown on the Banner Exchange network of web pages.

Link Exchange
http://www.linkexchange.com
Free banner advertising on over 250,000 web sites. Support for over 3,000 geographic regions and subject categories and over 30 languages. Reports and statistics about the people who visit your site.

Smart Clicks
http://www.smartclicks.com
Free banner exchange with automatic or manual targeting, animation allowed, real-time reporting and much more!

GSAnet
http://bs.gsanet.com
GSAnet Banner Swap is unique in that it offers up to a 1:1 display ratio to members depending on where you locate the banner on your web page(s). In addition, small sites (sites with few visitors) see an even greater ratio due to what is called "charity banners."

Link Media
http://www.linkmedia.com/network
LinkMedia Free Exchange is a free service for the Internet Community. As a member of the LinkMedia Free Exchange, you will receive free banner advertising on other member sites. In return, you will display banner ads on your site.

Associate and Affiliate Programs

AssociatePrograms
http://www.associateprograms.com
A large collection of valuable information and links related to companies that offer commission based advertising.

ClickTrade
http://www.clicktrade.com
Allows you to easily reward other web site owners for linking to your site by setting up your own link partner program. They also have several hundred sites that will pay you by the click for linking to them.

Refer-It
http://www.refer-it.com
A huge list of associate programs, where you get a percentage of sales coming from your site.

Banner Advertising Price Information

Ad Resource
http://www.adresource.com
Web advertising, marketing resources, and secrets. Ad Resource offers an extensive price guide about Internet advertising, including what the Top 100 sites are charging. This site also has a large number of web advertising related links.

Online Advertising Education

Website Promoters Resource Center
http://www.wprc.com
The focus of the Website Promoters Resource Center is to stay on the cutting edge of the developing web site promotion industry. If you are looking for resources to help conduct your own promotional campaign, or seek to hire a professional staff to conduct it for you, this is a good place to start.

Four Corners Effective Banners
http://www.whitepalm.com/fourcorners
This site is dedicated to the study of all things banner-like, including: banners, click-through ratios, banner advertising, banner link exchanging, etc. You'll learn how to improve your banners and increase your site traffic. And the best part, this entire site is free!

Mark Welch's Web Site Banner Advertising Site
http://www.markwelch.com/bannerad
A great site about ad networks, brokers, exchanges, pay-per-click and pay-per-sale (commission) ads, counters, trackers, software, and much more.

Advertising Age Magazine
http://adage.com/news_and_features/deadline
This advertising industry publication always has interesting articles on advertising online.

Internet Advertising Bureau - Online Advertising Effectiveness Study
http://www.mbinteractive.com/site/iab/study.html
The IAB Online Advertising Effectiveness Study is the most comprehensive and projectable test of online advertising effectiveness to date. With twelve major web sites and over 16,000 individual users taking part in the test, the study ranks as the largest, most rigorous test of advertising effectiveness conducted, to date, *in any medium.*

12

The Cybermall Advantage

Cybermalls are Internet shopping centers that contain "stores" related to a specific topic. Some of the more successful malls are those that concentrate on a specific type of product or service category. These cybermalls often do not bring in tremendous amounts of traffic but they do bring in targeted, interested people, looking for a specific type of product or service. The Hall of Malls is one site that provides a list of cybermalls you can search to determine if there are any that are appropriate for your company. In this chapter we cover:

- Can your site benefit from being linked in cybermalls?
- Cybermall features
- Types of cybermalls - which is best suited to your business?
- Where to look for cybermalls
- Discounts and coupons to lure customers
- Selecting the appropriate cybermall

- What will it cost?
- Checking visitor statistics

The Advantages of Internet Shopping Centers

Cybermalls are collections of commercial web sites on the Internet. There are literally thousands of cybermalls and they are increasingly growing in popularity. Cybermalls provide an arena where people can shop online via the Internet. Similar to traditional malls, cybermall merchants benefit by receiving more traffic due to the promotional power of, and services offered by, the mall owner. These malls are accessed by the consumer through a common Internet address.

Cyber-mall
An Internet shopping center

Some cybermalls will design, build, and host your web site, and offer ongoing maintenance of your site for a fee that is comparable to other web developers and service providers.

Other malls simply provide a link to your site on another server. If you already have a web site and choose this option the charges are generally a lot less.

When Are Cybermalls Appropriate?

There are many different reasons that businesses choose the cybermall route. Some businesses choose to participate in a cybermall and also offer their products or services from their own site. Some businesses choose to participate in a number of different cybermalls. Any one of the following may provide sound reasoning for their business decision.

- You don't have a credit card merchant account. Some financial institutions charge a premium for small business merchant accounts where the business is going to be selling online or they may even refuse to provide a merchant account for online vendors. The cybermall may provide merchant accounts or merchant account services to its tenants.

- You don't know how or don't have the time to work on building traffic to your site. In a cybermall the onus is on the mall to perform online and offline marketing activities to increase the traffic to their site. Your site will benefit from the general traffic that comes through the mall doors as long as your product is of interest to the incoming mall visitors.

Secure Server
A server allowing secure credit card transactions

- You don't have a secure server. The fact that a cybermall has a secure server may be reason enough to locate your online business there. If you are going to be selling online you need a **secure server** and the volume of business you are going to do may not warrant the purchase price and expertise required to set up your own secure server.

- You can locate your online storefront in a niche mall that caters to your target market.

E-Commerce
The buying and selling of goods and services on the Internet

- You don't have credit card validation. Many malls provide electronic commerce or **e-commerce** solutions for their tenants. Credit card validation online means that once the purchaser provides their credit card number as payment, the transaction is then authorized and approved by their financial institution. The transaction amount is automatically deposited into the bank account of the vendor, minus, of course, the credit card commission and usually the credit card validation charge.

- You don't have shopping cart capability. Shopping carts online allow a mall visitor to drop items into their shopping cart as they travel through an online store or cybermall with the click of their mouse. When they have finished their shopping they can review and edit their invoice online. They may decide they wanted two copies of that CD rather than one, and can make the change with one keystroke. Or they may delete a few items when they see that the total of the invoice is more than they were planning to spend. When the online invoice reflects exactly what they want, they complete the transaction by providing their credit card for payment. Where a business does not have the technical or financial resources to put shopping carts on their site, a cybermall might provide this valuable service.

Cybermall Categories

Cybermalls can be organized in a number of ways. These are described below.

Geographic Region

All of the tenants are located in the same geographic region. Many of these cybermalls are provided by an ISP for its clients. In many cases participation in these types of malls is done to provide easy access through a variety of means for the customer, to build name recognition with the local customer base, and as a means of advertising and cross-promotion.

Products and/or Services

All of the tenants provide similar types of products. These types of cybermalls are of interest to the same target market. A model airplane cybermall would consist of a number of merchants all providing products or services related to model airplanes. Other cybermalls that would fit into this category would be computer software cybermalls, electronics cybermalls, environmentally friendly products cybermalls, and vacation malls. Figures 12.1, 12.2, and 12.3 illustrate some of the cybermalls available.

Industry

All of the tenants would be in the same industry. A financial services industry cybermall would provide a wide range of different products and services from insurance products and services, banking products and services, investment products and services, and accounting services and products.

Unrelated Products and Services Catering to One Demographic

Some cybermalls have tenants that provide a variety of unrelated products and services. There should always be some common theme that

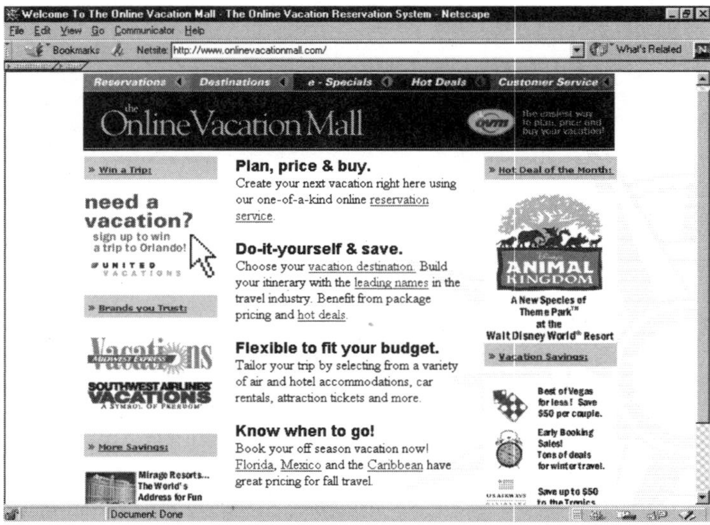

Figure 12.1. Online Vacation Mall allows you to order airline tickets, make hotel reservations, book your car rental, and order attraction tickets from one location.

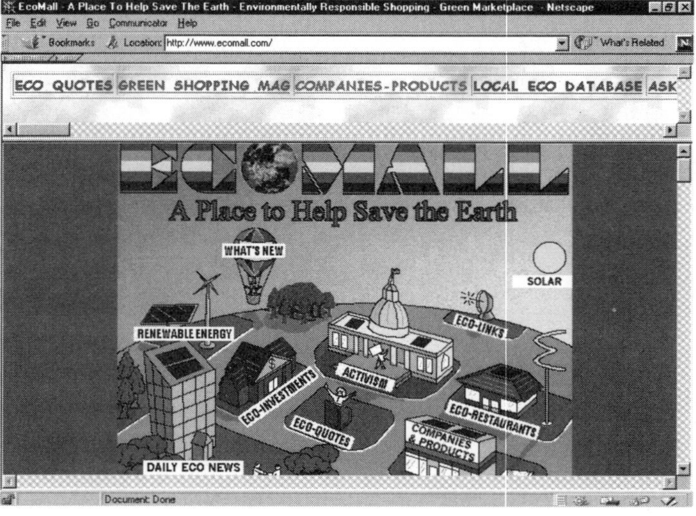

Figure 12.2. EcoMall provides you with everything green.

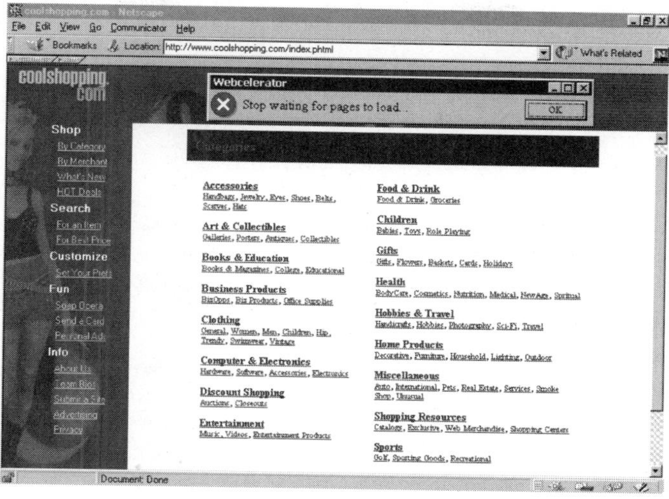

Figure 12.3. *coolshopping.com* is a general mall offering everything from candy to cars.

ties the visitors together for target marketing purposes. A children's cybermall that has vendors providing everything from clothing to books to gifts to toys would be a good examples of this type of cybermall. A senior's cybermall could include a wide range of very different products and services of interest to that demographic.

Typical Cybermall Products and Services

Most of the items you would find in your local shopping malls are appropriate for a cybermall. Some items that are not typically found in retail shopping centers because of the space requirements, like car dealerships, are also appropriate for cybermalls. Products and services that are popular in cybermalls today include:

- Software
- Books

- Computers
- Electronics
- Gifts
- Games
- Clothing
- Travel
- Arts and collectibles
- Automotive
- Food
- Health and fitness
- Housewares
- Financial products and services
- Professional services
- Sports and recreation
- Specialty shops

Some malls choose to concentrate on a specific niche, such as the one shown in Figure 12.4. The niche can be a type of product or service category. These malls bring in very targeted, interested people looking for a specific type of product or service. There are a number of cybermalls focusing on niche categories such as new automobiles, used automobiles, antique or collector automobiles, environmentally friendly products, tourist resorts, electronics, magazines, coins, stamps, and software.

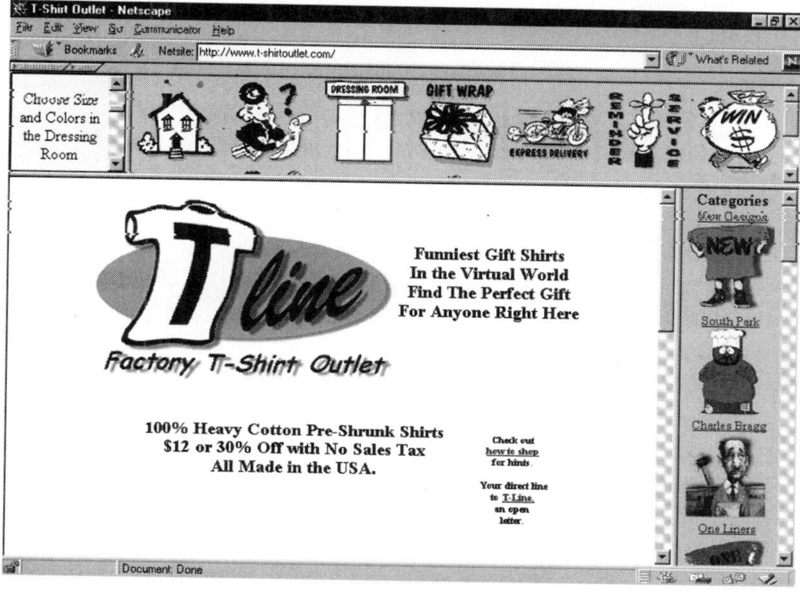

Figure 12.4. The Factory T-Shirt Outlet is a storefront that focuses on one product but provides a range of services such as gift wrap, delivery, and a dressing room.

Selecting the Right Cybermall

Before you commit to a cybermall that is going to host your site you should check out a number of things in your evaluation process. Choosing a successful mall is tricky but if you use the following guidelines you will be better equipped to make the right decision.

High Speed Access

The cybermall merchant should have connection through T1 or ISDN lines. If access is slow, the visitors will not wait. This is very similar to traditional retail outlets. If the line up at the cash register is too long, customers will not wait and will shop elsewhere.

Home Page and Interface

A good cybermall should have a good quality, attractive home page with consistent navigation throughout the site.

Domain Name

The mall you choose should have a logical and easy-to-remember domain name.

Hardware

The cybermall's server should be reliable, state-of-the-art, fast, and have lots of capacity to handle the anticipated volume. There should be technicians available to provide technical support and quickly resolve any problems that occur.

Categories

Before choosing a mall, make sure that your business fits within one of the categories in the mall. Don't join a mall that is targeting a different demographic than yours.

Online and Offline Promotion

Make sure that the mall you choose is promoted both online and offline. Many of the malls only promote online. The cybermall owner should be able to provide you with details of their Internet marketing strategy to increase the traffic of their targeted market to their site.

Site Maintenance Activities

Successful web sites must be updated on a continual basis. Ensure that the mall provides software tools to make it easy for you to maintain your own site or, if the mall provides the updates, that their fees regarding changes are not too expensive.

Traffic

Obtain details on mall traffic and the number of unique visitors to the home page of the mall, if possible. Any other count of hits may include hits to the pages of merchants in the mall, which would be misleading. Talk with other merchants residing in the mall about their traffic, as well as their experience with the mall itself (fee increases, hidden costs, server downtime, etc.). Many progressive malls now provide their tenants with access to their web traffic analysis.

Secure Server

Ensure that the mall has a secure server allowing you to offer secure credit card sales transactions. Most consumers will not purchase online without it.

Credit Card Merchant Account

Merchant accounts for the popular credit cards are usually difficult to obtain for businesses with only a virtual presence. If you don't have a merchant account, you will want to choose a mall that offers this service.

Promotions

Find out what type of promotional efforts the mall is involved in. Many malls indicate that they promote extensively but ensure they are actually targeting shoppers *not merchants*.

Commission Fees

Some malls charge a commission on every sale. Check the details on all commissions, transaction fees, and other charges. If the mall is responsible for all the traffic to your site they should be compensated for this activity either through your monthly rental charge or a commission on sales. If you are making an effort to promote your site yourself and the traffic to your site is a result of your marketing efforts, it is unreasonable for the mall to expect to be compensated for each and every transaction on your site.

Cybermall History and Reputation

Find out how long the mall has been in existence. Talk to existing tenants and past tenants about their experience.

Other Features and Services Provided by the Cybermall

Cybermalls may include a variety of other products and services to their tenants, similar to Figure 12.5. When comparing cybermalls make sure you are comparing apples with apples. Some additional features and services provided by cybermalls might include the supply of mailing lists, supply of autoresponders, or provision of chat rooms, and bulletin boards.

Cybermall Features

Cybermalls may provide a number of features to their tenants as well as to the tenant's customers:

Electronic Shopping Carts

Shopping carts, like the one shown in Figure 12.6, are relatively new to the Internet. They enable users to click on items they would like to purchase from various mall vendors and put them in their shopping cart. At the end of their online shopping trip they have an opportunity to review the contents of their cart as well as the invoice. Purchases can be edited before an order is placed.

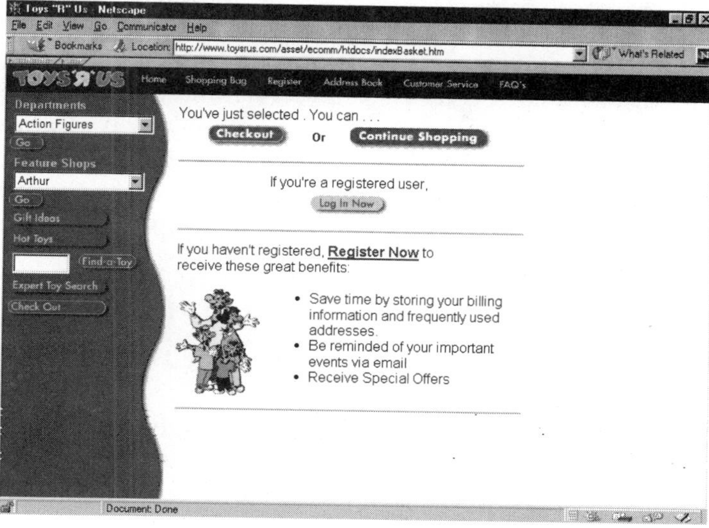

Figure 12.5. Toys R Us allows you to register your billing information and ship to addresses to expedite your check-out process.

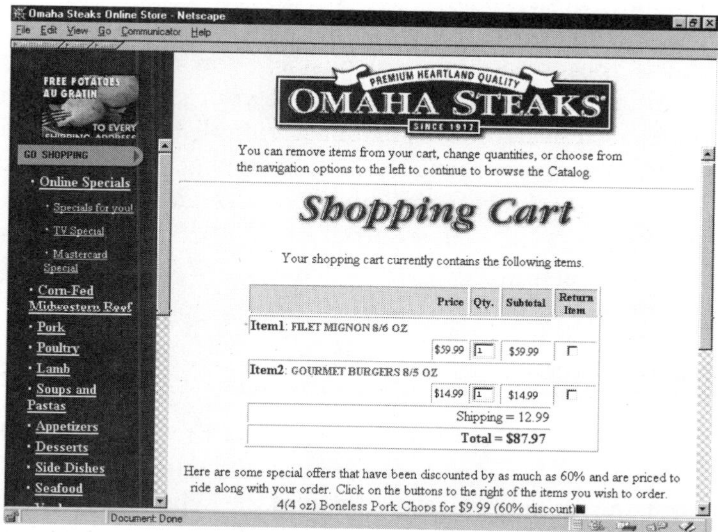

Figure 12.6. Omaha Steaks provides a shopping cart to facilitate your purchase.

Secure Ordering

Most cybermalls offer a secure server and encrypted transactions for their tenant's online transactions. Technology is advancing rapidly in the area of e-commerce and the cybermalls are among the first web sites on the Internet to make use of the latest capabilities. Some malls now offer online charge card authorization and automatic deposit for their tenants.

Search Capabilities

Many cybermalls will provide a site search capability to assist shoppers with finding the items they are looking for.

More than One Cybermall?

It may be appropriate to join more than one cybermall especially if you have your own site and are just paying a monthly fee for the link from your storefront in the mall to your site. If you decide that this is appropriate for your business you should have some mechanism in place to track the traffic to your site to determine which malls are effective. This can be accomplished quite easily these days with all the web traffic analysis tools that are available. Web Crumbs, available from ThinWeb, *http://www.thinweb.com,* is a powerful traffic analysis program.

Cybermall Pricing

Malls charge their tenants in a variety of ways. If you choose a mall that hosts one page as a storefront and a link from that storefront to your site on a different server than the cybermall, the charge is generally a flat fee per month. If your web site is hosted by the cybermall you may be charged on a flat fee basis or your charge may be a basic fee with add-ons or you may be charged on a commission-on-sales basis. The variable charges are generally either on a commission or set fee per transaction basis.

Cybermall charges can be anywhere from $25 a month to be linked to their storefront—to over $1,000 a month, which includes services and a number of features provided by the host.

Where to Look for Cybermalls

A number of these meta-indexes of cybermalls can be found online. There are cybermall web rings that can be researched and also cybermalls of cybermalls. There are all kinds of locations and sites listed at the end of this chapter in the Internet Resources to assist you in finding the appropriate cybermall for your business.

Enticing Customers with Coupons and Discounts

To increase the traffic to your cybermall site you can post coupons either as banner ads or links from other sites. The sites you choose to host these banner ads or links should be those that appeal to your target market or you might consider purchasing a keyword from a search engine. See Chapter 11 for advice on appropriate banner advertising.

You can also use online coupons, which can be printed from your site, to increase the traffic to your offline locations. If your customers know they can check your weekly coupons or sales it will encourage repeat visits from your target customers.

You might also consider trading coupons with other online vendors who offer noncompeting products to the same target market.

Internet Resources for Chapter 12

The Most Frequently Shopped Malls On the Internet
http://ourworld.compuserve.com/homepages/asappub/CYBER.HTM
Listing the more commonly visited cybermalls on the Internet.

The Hall of Malls
http://nsns.com/MouseTracks/HallofMalls.html
The most comprehensive listing of all known online malls located on the Net.

MallPark
http://www2.mallpark.com
Thousands of online merchants by shopping category! Instant searching. Secure order forms, shopping carts, merchant accounts to accept credit cards, and merchants can link for free.

The Cybermall.com Directory
http://www.cybermall.com
Evaluation of hundreds of online malls and selection of only what they determine are the very best. Malls cannot purchase a listing on this site (unlike other directories) and are selected exclusively because they provide you with a positive home shopping experience. You get access to the better shopping malls without fighting through hundreds of them. Their categorical listings include brief site reviews to help you find the quality shopping sites you want without all the work.

Malls.com
http://malls.com
Besides providing a range of products and services from their mall, Malls.com provides a huge meta-index of all the malls on the Net at *http://malls.com/metalist.html*. This list is a great starting point when doing your cybermall research.

eMall
http://www.emall.com
This is a great location for organic and natural foods. They have a Complete Health Online Store, a Spice Merchant section with the flavors of Asia, fine teas, and sun roasted Mexican coffees.

ShopNow Market
http://www.internet-mall.com
ShopNow Market's Merchandising Program gives you two key components to successful online marketing: strategic positioning and targeted, focused traffic generation programs. You'll benefit from their partner-

ships with high-traffic sites such as Yahoo! and PC World as well as from an aggressive advertising and marketing campaign designed to drive hordes of shoppers to this portal—and to your business. They provide Merchant Listings with options ranging anywhere from an Entry Tenant position with a listing on the department level for just $25 a year—to virtually owning the category with top-level placement and other "spotlight" positioning as a $995 per month Anchor Tenant. They provide a'la carte programs for banner, sponsorship, and e-mail advertising. They also offer sponsorship and promotional packages.

Internet Plaza
http://internet-plaza.net
This site is actually a "cybertown" with addresses for each category of product/service they provide. They have Card and Gift Drive, Fashion Blvd., Finance Street, Home and Garden Row, Career Way, Sport and Recreation Street, Travel Avenue, Book End, Gourmet Lane, Health Care Place, Impression Avenue, Industry Parkway and Kids Alley. Neat site!

Access Market Square
http://www.icw.com/mall.html
Access Market Square has an Occasion (birthday, anniversary, etc.) reminder service that also provides personalized gift ideas. They also have a great search engine that allows you to enter names of items, brandnames, product types, or store names. They provide a wide variety of products by category including art, audio-video, automotive, books, clothes, computers, electronics, flowers, food, health, jewelry, music, sports, travel, and others. Access Market Square uses VeriSign for secure ordering capabilities.

American Shopping Mall
http://www.greenearth.com
The American Shopping Mall has been rated among the topmost visited sites on the Internet by *PC Magazine.* They profess to be one of the busiest virtual shopping malls on the World Wide Web with over 32 million visitors last year and over 50 million visitors since their opening in 1995.

iMall
http://www.imall.com

This is an electronic commerce enabler of small and medium-sized businesses allowing them to cost-effectively engage in electronic commerce through the use of iMALL's proprietary e-commerce tools and services. iMALL offers its electronic commerce services directly to merchants, as well as through partnerships with leading ISPs, Web hosting firms, and financial service companies with an Internet focus. The company professes to operate the largest shopping mall on the Internet, with more than 1,600 hosted storefronts, and millions of visitors monthly.

Branch Mall
http://branch.com
Branch Mall provides a search engine for visitors. Their categories include sports and recreation, travel and leisure, gift shop, book store, furniture store, flower shop, clothing, computing, business and career, and real estate and home.

FactoryMall.com
http://www.factorymall.com/default.htm?loc=5
FactoryMall.com professes to be the leading online retailer of brand name merchandise. Use their Quick Search feature to find a product or brand, or simply click on Directory to view FactoryMall's shopping departments. Sign up for free membership to receive special savings and other exciting benefits. Use their Live Chat Personal Shopper service to obtain personal online assistance. Representatives are available during normal business hours. If you would prefer to speak to someone in person, you are provided with their I-800 number.

13

Keep 'Em Coming Back

There are many little things that will spice up your web site to "keep 'em coming back." Learn the tips, tools, and techniques to get visitors to return to your site again and again. In this chapter we cover:

- Attractive web site content
- Have your own "What's New Page," "Tip of the Day," and "Awards Page"
- Customer employment opportunities
- Hosting online seminars
- Ensuring you are bookmarked
- Cartoons, contests, jokes, and trivia
- Calendar of events and reminder services
- Interesting bulletin boards
- Online chat sessions, workshops, and discussion groups

- Special guests or celebrity appearances
- Giveaways, awards, and surveys
- Offline tactics for promotion

Encourage Repeat Visits

Just as you would want customers to visit your place of business frequently, so too in cyberspace you want customers and potential customers to visit often.

Use a "What's New Page" for Repeat Hits

A What's New Page can mean different things to different sites. For some, this page updates the users with the summaries of the most recent features and additions to a particular site, as in Figure 13.1. For others, What's New may be What's New in their industry or What's New in their product line. If visitors repeatedly find interesting additions in the What's New section, in whatever context you use it, they will come back to your site on a regular basis to check out what's new.

Free Stuff—Everyone Loves It

Giving items away for free is a great way to increase traffic—everybody likes a freebie. If you give something away each week, you are sure to have a steady stream of repeat traffic. When you have freebies or giveaways on your site, your pages can be listed and linked from the many sites on the Internet that list places people can receive free stuff.

If you want to bring only people from your target market to your site, then don't give away mainstream things like screen savers, shareware games, utilities, etc. Try to give away something that only people interested in your industry would want.

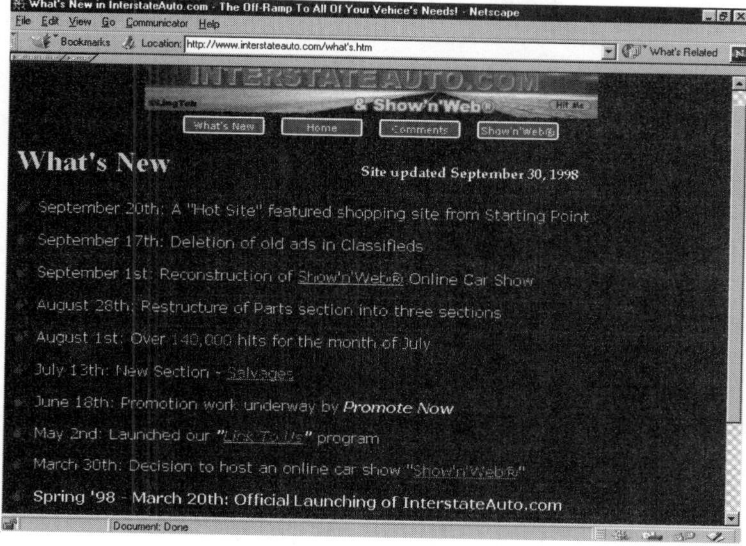

Figure 13.1. *InterstateAuto.com*'s What's New Page gives a chronology of updates and changes to their site. A visitor can quickly see what has changed on the site since their last visit.

If you don't care what traffic comes your way, and any traffic is good traffic, then give away useful things that everybody needs. Try to have your logo and URL displayed on the item. For example, a neat screen saver can be made that displays your logo and URL. When this is made available as a download, there are no handling or shipping charges associated with it. If your freebie is something that has your URL on it and is something that is generally kept around a computer it reminds and encourages people to visit your site. A mousepad with your URL would be a good example.

Give a Taste of Your Product with Sample Give-Aways

Use a traditional marketing approach and give away free samples of your product from your web site, as shown in Figure 13.2. After giving away the samples, follow up with an e-mail. Ask the people

Figure 13.2. Sweet 'N Low offers a free sample from their web site.

who received a sample what they thought of it, if they had any problems, and if they have any questions. Direct the samplers back to your web site for more information and discounts on purchasing the regular version of the product.

Resisting a Deal Is Hard with Coupons and Discounts

Offer coupons and discount vouchers that can be printed from your site. You can change the coupon daily or weekly to encourage repeat visits. People will come back to your site again and again if they know they will find good deals there. This is a great strategy to use in conjunction with a free sample give-away. If people liked the sample, give them a coupon and they may purchase the regular version at a discount. If they like the regular version, they may purchase it again at full price or recommend the product to a friend.

You can develop a coupon banner ad, shown in Figure 13.3, which links to your site where the coupon can be printed. The banner ads should be placed on sites frequented by your target market.

You can trade coupons with non-competing sites that target the same market that you do. Your coupon on their site links to your site, and their coupon on your site links to their site.

There are meta-indexes to sites with coupons or discounts from which you can be linked for greater exposure.

A Calendar of Events Keeps Visitors Informed

A comprehensive, current calendar of events related to your company or your industry will encourage repeat visits. A sample calendar is shown in Figure 13.4. Your calendar should always be kept up to date and be of value to your readers. A calendar of events for a band might show their scheduled appearances.

Figure 13.3. The Coupon-Pages! provides a list of local and national coupons. You can bet they see a lot of repeat visitors!

Figure 13.4. Puppyworks provides a calendar of educational dog events–seminars, conferences, trade shows, and special events.

Lure Customers with Contests and Competitions

Contests and competitions are great traffic builders. Some sites hold regular contests on a weekly or monthly basis to generate repeat visitors. Holding contests is also a great way to find out about your target market by requesting information on the entry form.

What type of contest you hold depends upon your Internet marketing objectives. If you want to attract as many people as possible to your site regardless of who they are, then offer items such as money, trips, cars, computers, etc. as in Figure 13.5. If you would like to attract potential customers from your target market, then give away something that relates to your products and industry.

To enter the contest you could simply request that people fill out an electronic ballot including their name, address, phone number, and e-mail address. If you want to find out something about the people entering, ask them to answer a question about your products. If the prize is one of your products, ask entrants to write a short essay

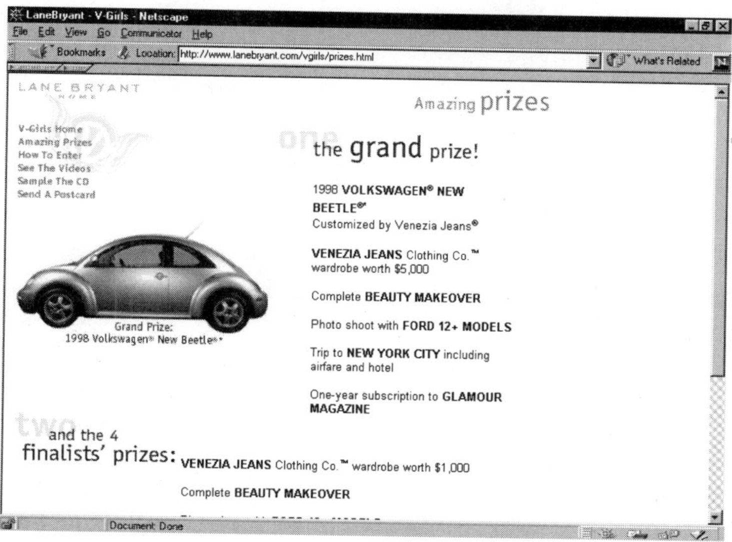

Figure 13.5. Lane Bryant sure does have amazing prizes!

outlining why they would like to have the product you are giving away. You can award the winner or winners with the product and follow up with the other entrants. These people may be in a position to buy your products and you will have gained some valuable knowledge from the essays submitted.

You can turn a contest into a competition. If your web site relates to cooking or baking, ask entrants to submit their best recipe using your food product. People will visit your site to see the winning recipes and you may get some ideas for future marketing efforts. Other competitions may include things like best photo with product X, best short story about product X, best drawing of product X, etc. This creates better brand awareness and reinforces sales of your product. The closer the contest relates to your product, the better.

Instead of offering just one prize, offer a number of smaller prizes as well. This makes the odds look better and people feel they have a better chance of winning.

Before you go ahead with holding any kind of contest check out all of the legal issues. There may be restrictions that you don't know about; e.g., you may be required to purchase a legal permit to hold lotteries.

Using Employment Opportunities to Increase Visitors

People involved in a job search or interested in new job opportunities will revisit your site occasionally to see your list of available positions. See Figure 13.6 for a sample employment page.

Create Useful Links from Your Site

Provide visitors with links to other sites similar to yours. Do not put outbound links on your home page. Place them down a level or two after the visitors have seen all the information you may have to offer before you provide the links away from your site. Try exchanging links with others so you receive a link to your site. As long as your links are of value to your visitors, people will come back to see if you have found any new and interesting sites for them to visit.

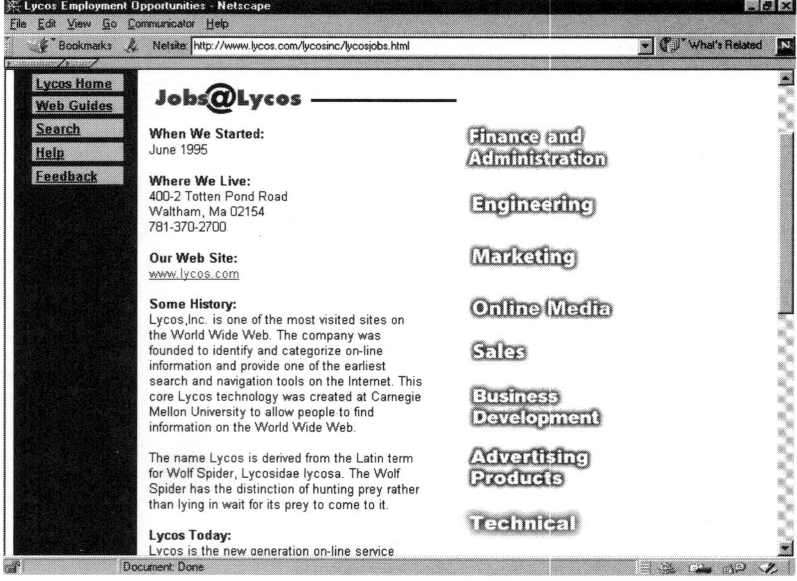

Figure 13.6. Lycos provides information on employment opportunities in their *Jobs@Lycos* section.

Investing in Online Chat Sessions

Chat rooms are very popular (Figure 13.7) and, to some, even addictive. If you have a chat forum on your site, make sure the topic relates to your business. To encourage repeat visitors you could change the topic from day to day or week to week. You could also have celebrity appearances in your chat sessions.

Providing Tip of the Day to Encourage Repeat Visits

Have a section that offers cool tips that relate to your business, as in Figure 13.8. These tips can be one sentence to one paragraph long. If visitors find your advice helpful they will return repeatedly to see what interesting piece of information you have displayed that day.

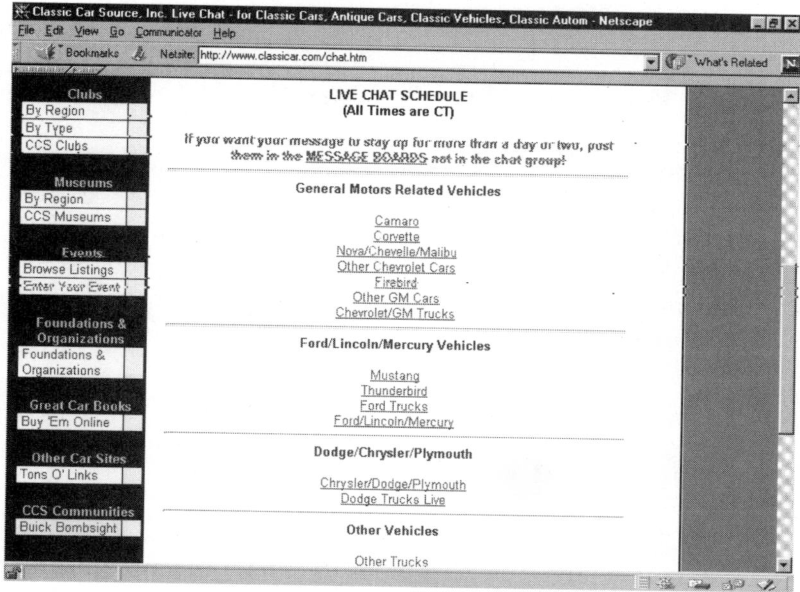

Figure 13.7. Live chats are becoming very popular. *Classicar.com* provides a number of live chats, each related to a specific type of vehicle.

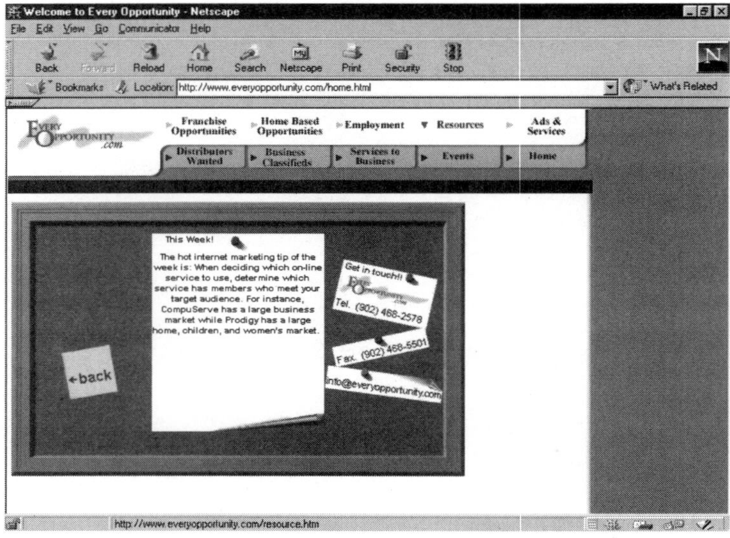

Figure 13.8 Everyopportunity.com provides an *Internet Marketing Tip of the Week.*

Ensuring Your Site Gets Bookmarked

Encourage visitors to add you to their bookmark list. Somewhere on your site display "Bookmark me now!" (see Figure 13.9). A call to action is often effective. Make sure the title of the page that has the "Bookmark me now!" clearly identifies your site and its contents in an enticing way as the title is what will appear in the bookmark file as a description.

World Interaction with Bulletin Boards

It can be very satisfying to see people join in from all over the world just to interact with each other about a topic that relates to your web site, as shown in Figure 13.10. Beware, you will have to keep an eye on the messages and may even have to play referee occasionally.

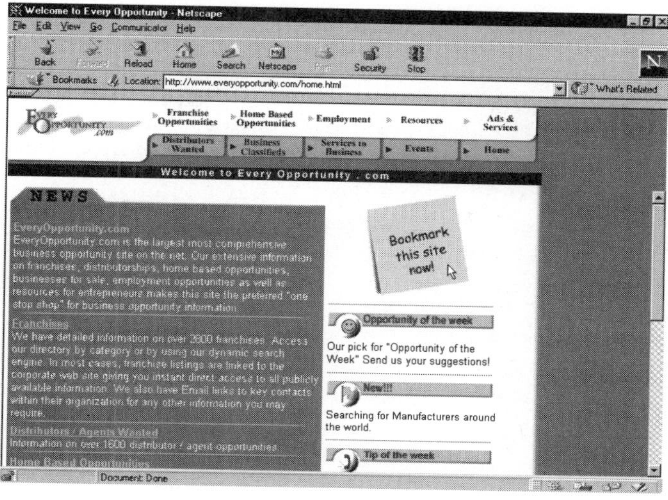

Figure 13.9. When you see a "Bookmark this site now!" call to action, nine times out of ten you will at least consider it.

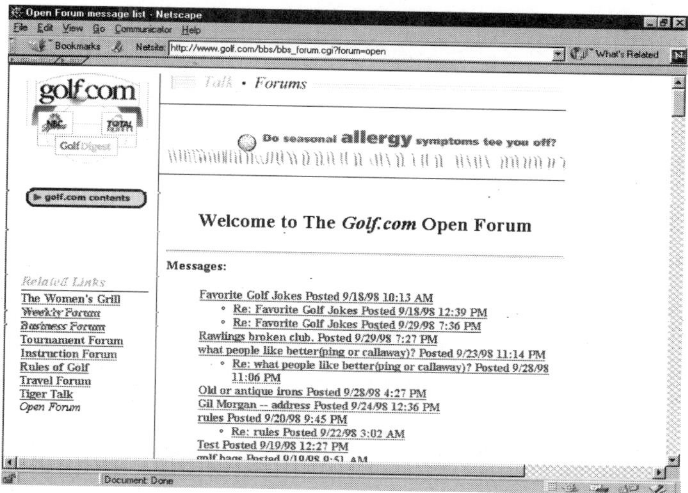

Figure 13.10. Golf.com provides a number of forums or discussion groups related to golf topics. They provide business, tournament, instruction, and travel forums.

Inviting Visitors to Contribute with Surveys

Performing surveys is a great way to increase the traffic to your site. In order for people to want to fill out the survey and see the results, the survey topic must be interesting. To encourage input, the survey results might only be available to participants.

Your survey could be on a topic concerning current events or something pertaining to your industry. The more controversial or debatable the topic of the survey, the more people will visit to contribute or see the results. If you want to draw a very targeted audience, pick a topic that would be interesting to that market alone.

In performing these surveys you are building repeat traffic and you are gathering valuable information on your market. If you hold an interesting survey every week or every month, then you will be sure to retain a loyal audience of repeat visitors. If your surveys are newsworthy, then you can send out press releases to publicize the results and gain publicity for your site.

Your surveys should be short and to the point. Let people know why you are asking visitors to do the survey and when the deadline is. Make your questions clear and concise. The responses should be Yes/No or multiple choice.

When reporting the results don't just put them on your web page. Post the results to newsgroups and mailing lists that would be interested. Don't forget to add your sig. file. If you are holding weekly or monthly surveys, let people know via your sig. file what the next survey topic will be and that there is more information on your web site.

Encourage Repeat Visits with Your "Site of the Day"

Having your own "Site of the Day" or "Site of the Week" listing as in Figure 13.11, will mean a lot of work, searching the Internet for a cool site to add, or looking through all the submissions. However, if your picks are interesting to your audience, you may find that avid Internet users come back every day to see what great new site is listed. Remember that this must be updated on schedule; displaying a week-old "Site of the Day" will reflect poorly on your site and your company.

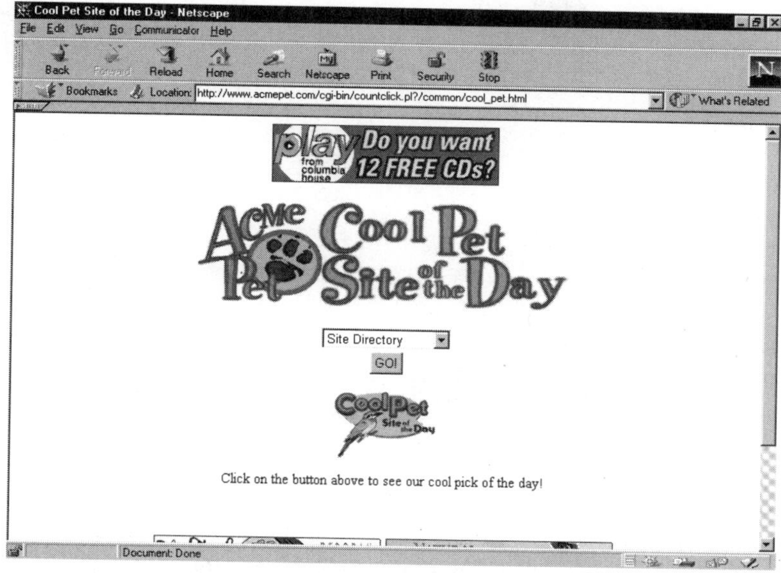

Figure 13.11. Acme Pet provides a Cool Pet Site of the Day.

Keep Them Happy with Cartoons

Displaying relevant cartoons keeps your site dynamic and fun. You do not necessarily have to create all of the content and features yourself.

Sending Postcards Around the Internet

Visitors can create original postcards that can be e-mailed to their family and friends. The postcards should be able to be identified as coming from your site—have your logo and URL displayed somewhere on them. I can't begin to count the number of beautiful cards I have received via e-mail from my 11, 10, and 8 year-olds, each with a beautiful verse, and complete with audio and video. The cards have come via the Blue Mountain Card site (see Figure 13.12) and, yes, I

Figure 13.12. Blue Mountain Arts allows you to personalize and send via e-mail their audio and video greeting cards.

have noticed that my recent offline card purchases have happened to be from the same company.

Benefiting from Humor with Jokes and Trivia

"Laughter is the best medicine" and could prove to be a popular feature of your web page, as in Figure 13.13. People enjoy trivia, or a "thought of the day," and there are many sources for you to draw from. Be sure and update regularly.

Who Doesn't Love Games?

More and more sites are featuring fun activities and games on their sites. (A sample game site is shown in Figure 13.14.) Just about any-

Figure 13.13. Allworld Internet Services provides a Joke of the Day. They also provide a Daily Inspiration.

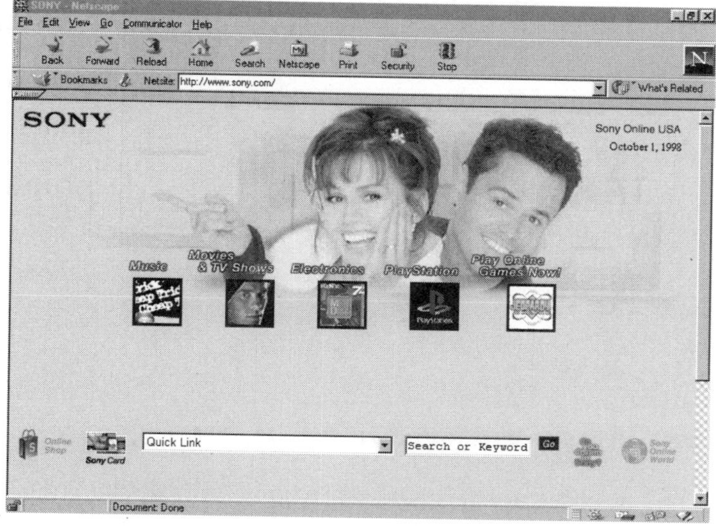

Figure 13.14. Sony provides a section for playing online games that sees a lot of repeat traffic.

thing goes here. You can host anything from a Star Wars trivia contest to having guests play an interactive graphical game with other visitors.

Keep Customers In Touch with Update Reminders

Have an e-mail submit link on your page which people will join if they want to be notified of any updates or content changes to your pages. This is similar to a mailing list except you only write to the "list" when changes have been made. This is effective when you have a Newsletter or a frequently visited Calendar of Events on your site.

Special Events Reminder Services

People can sign up to be reminded of something via e-mail on specified dates (see Figure 13.15). This feature was originally thought of by a florist to remind people about important dates. You can remind people about any number of things relating to your business. If you own a site that sells fishing and hunting gear, you could get people to sign up to be reminded when certain fishing or hunting seasons start. You should try to develop a reminder service that relates to something that you sell from your site. In your reminder you can include suggestions about what fishing fly works best at this time of the year or what item from your inventory would be great to give as a gift on Mother's Day.

Adding Image with Advice Columns

Some web sites are incorporating advice columns, as in Figure 13.16. People will return again and again to read the e-mails asking for advice and the responses that are given. This also helps perpetuate an image of your company as an expert in your given field.

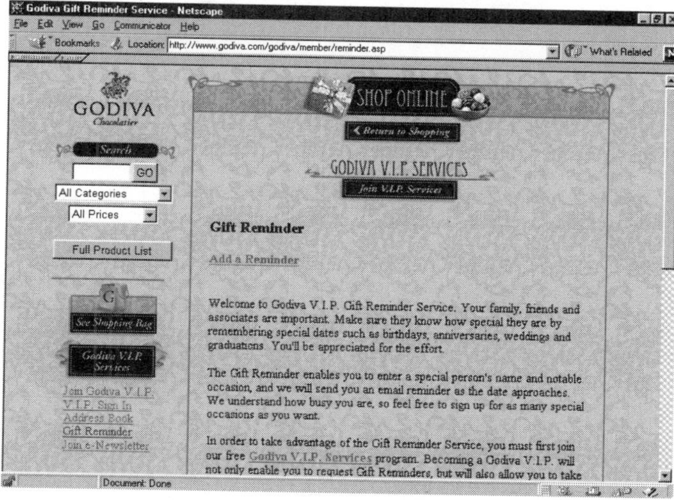

Figure 13.15. Godiva provides a gift reminder service. No excuses to ever forget an anniversary or birthday again!

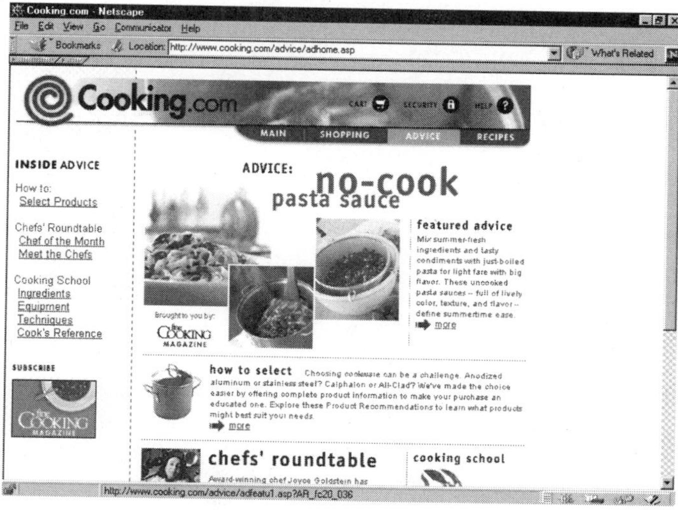

Figure 13.16. Cooking.com has an advice section where selected requests are posted as featured advice.

Internet Resources for Chapter 13

More Hits for Your WWW Site
http://www.adze.com/zine/morehits.html
Teachings on "How to get people to keep coming back to your site."

Web Developers Virtual Library
http://www.stars.com
A comprehensive illustrated encyclopedia of web technology, the WDVL is for webmasters and Internet developers. It's a well-organized gold mine of tutorials, demos, and links to great resources.

10 Secrets of the Web Masters
http://www.i-strategies.com/10secret.html
A guide to web design and strategy to get visitors and make them return.

Guide to Web Style
http://www.sun.com/styleguide
Sun Microsystem's cookbook for better web site design to encourage repeat visitors.

Keep 'em Coming Back!
http://www.webmaster-resources.com/guest11.shtml
Everything you need to build, maintain, and promote a successful web site. Articles, reviews, design guidelines, and over a thousand organized links to resources around the Internet. The one-stop shop for web masters.

Design Tips

Five Most Serious Web Design Errors
http://www.hp.com/Ebusiness/webdesign.html
Web designer tips to avoid fatal flaws that could cause your site to fail.

Yale Style Manual-Table of Contents
http://info.med.yale.edu/caim/manual/contents.html
A good example of a detailed web design manual to keep visitors coming back.

Web Architect
http://argus-inc.com/design/webarch.html
Archive of Web Review site design features to help you get the perfect layout.

Web Page Design - Introduction
http://www.wpdfd.com
Web design from the perspective of typography and graphics to keep visitors happy; no HTML.

Pulling the Plug-Ins
http://www.cio.com/archive/webbusiness/060198_main_content.html
Web plug-ins are finally on the outs with web designers. So how should you cram all that interactivity in your web pages without alienating your visitors? Go here and find out.

HTML Design Tips
http://stoopidsoftware.com/tips
HTML tips and quick answers to common web-related questions, including how to get your visitors to return.

Conservatism of Web Users
http://www.useit.com/alertbox/980322.html
Statistics show that web users are adopting new web technologies at slower rates, affecting how you should design your site.

Features - how to - elements of web design
http://www.builder.com/Graphics/Design
CNET's elements of good web design to help in your web page design.

What I Learned Judging the @d:Tech Awards
http://www.o-a.com/adtech.Chicago/adtechChig—floor9.html
Cliff Kurtzman's insights as a judge of good and bad web site design.

14

Maximizing Media Relations

Your online media strategy can be extremely effective in building traffic to your site. Press release distribution can be done easily. Build the right list of e-mail addresses or make use of one of the online press distribution services. Most reporters and writers have e-mail addresses. Some do not like to receive e-mailed press releases while others prefer e-mail versions. When e-mail press releases are sent out reporters will reply by e-mail; they will expect your response within 24 hours. Develop a media kit that you can e-mail out to editors. In this chapter we cover:

- Developing your online media strategy
- Public relations vs. advertising
- Online public relations vs. traditional public relations
- Effective press releases
- Press release and distribution services online
- How to distribute press releases online

- Providing a page for media on your site
- How to find reporters online
- How reporters want to receive your information
- Encourage re-publication of your article with a direct link to your site or article
- Providing press kits online
- Electronic newsletters
- Resources

Managing Effective Public Relations

Press release distribution can be accomplished easily, if you have an established list of reporters and editors, or if you make use of a press distribution service.

Media relations are very important to your marketing efforts. The best results are achieved when you integrate both online and offline publicity campaigns.

Maintaining effective public relations will deliver a number of benefits to your company. Your company and products can be given exposure through press releases and a positive image for your company will be portrayed. Your relationship with current customers will be reinforced and new relationships will be formed.

Benefits of Publicity vs. Advertising

Media coverage, or *publicity*, has a major advantage over paid advertisements. Articles written by a reporter carry more weight with the public than do ads. This is because the media and reporters are seen as unbiased third parties. Articles printed in media publications are given more credibility by the public than advertisements.

Another advantage of distributing press releases is that it is more cost effective than advertising. You have to pay for advertising space on a web site or time on the radio, but the costs are minimal when writing and distributing press releases.

One of the disadvantages of press releases vs. advertising is that you don't have control over what is published. If the editor decides to cast your company in a negative light, then there is nothing you can do to stop him or her. If the writer of the piece does not like your company, for whatever reason, this may come across in the article. Basically, after your press release is distributed you have no control over what will be written about your company.

It is important to note that when generating publicity, you may lose control over the timing of your release. For example, you may want an article released the day before your big sale but the editor relegates it to a date the following week. There is nothing you can do about this. It is not a good idea to rely exclusively on publicity for important or newsworthy events because if the release is not reviewed and considered newsworthy, you may be stuck with no promotion at all.

What Is a Press Release?

Before you begin your media campaign you should know what press releases are and how to write them. Press releases are designed to inform reporters of events concerning your company that the public may consider newsworthy. Press releases can get your company free public attention. A press release is a standard form of communication with the media. Press releases must contain newsworthy information. Companies that continually send worthless information in a blatant attempt to get their name in the press will not establish a good relationship with the media.

Writing a Press Release

Your press release should follow a standard format, which is described in the following paragraphs.

Notice of Release

The first thing the reader sees should be:

FOR IMMEDIATE RELEASE

Unless you have sent the information in advance of the time you would like it published. In that case state it as follows:

FOR RELEASE: Wednesday, April 14, 1999 (using the date you want it released.)

Remember that no matter what date you put here the publication can release the information before or after the specified date. If the news is really big it is not likely that the publication will hold it until the date you have specified.

Header

The header should be in the upper-left corner. It should contain all of the contact information for one or two key people. These contacts should be able to answer any questions regarding the press release. If the reporter cannot get in touch with someone to answer their questions, then they may print incorrect information or even drop the article all together.

Connex Network Incorporated
Suite 110
800 Windmill Road
Dartmouth, Nova Scotia
Canada B3B 1L1
Tel 902-468-2578 Fax 902-468-2233
Contact: Susan Sweeney

Headline

Your headline should summarize your message and make the reader want to continue reading.

City and Date

Name the city you are reporting from and the date you wrote the press release.

The Body

Your first sentence within the body of the press release should sum up your headline and immediately inform the reader as to why this is newsworthy. With the number of press releases reporters receive, if you don't grab their attention immediately they won't read your release. Begin by listing all of the most relevant information first, leaving the supporting information last.

Ask yourself the 5 Ws (who, what, where, when, and why) and answer them up front. Write the press release just as if you were writing a newspaper article for publication. Include some quotes from key individuals in your company and any other relevant outside sources that are credible. If there are any statistics that support your main message, include them as well. Your last paragraph should be a short company description.

The Close

If your release is two pages long, center the word "-more-" at the bottom of the first page. To end your release, there are three ways of standard notation to do this: center the symbol "#," the word "end," or the number "-30-" at the end of your message.

A sample press release is shown in Figure 14.1.

Advantages of Interactive Press Releases

Online press releases take the same standard format as offline press releases but the online press release can be interactive with links to a variety of interesting information that supports your message. Reporters can easily find out other facts by following your links. Additional items included in your interactive press releases are:

- Links to the e-mail addresses of contact people

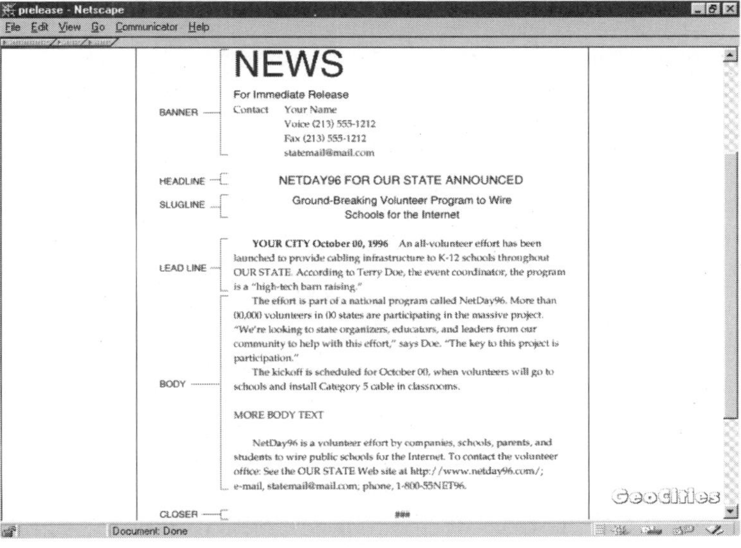

NEWS

For Immediate Release

Contact Your Name
Voice (213) 555-1212
Fax (213) 555-1212
statemail@mail.com

NETDAY96 FOR OUR STATE ANNOUNCED

Ground-Breaking Volunteer Program to Wire Schools for the Internet

YOUR CITY October 00, 1996 An all-volunteer effort has been launched to provide cabling infrastructure to K-12 schools throughout OUR STATE. According to Terry Doe, the event coordinator, the program is a "high-tech barn raising."

The effort is part of a national program called NetDay96. More than 00,000 volunteers in 00 states are participating in the massive project. "We're looking to state organizers, educators, and leaders from our community to help with this effort," says Doe. "The key to this project is participation."

The kickoff is scheduled for October 00, when volunteers will go to schools and install Category 5 cable in classrooms.

MORE BODY TEXT

NetDay96 is a volunteer effort by companies, schools, parents, and students to wire public schools for the Internet. To contact the volunteer office: See the OUR STATE Web site at http://www.netday96.com/; e-mail, statemail@mail.com; phone, 1-800-55NET96.

###

Figure 14.1. A sample online press release.

- A link to the company web page
- Links to articles and related issues both on the corporate web site and on other sites as well
- Links to graphics and pictures for illustration
- Links to key corporate player biographies and photos

Sending Press Releases on Your Own vs. Using a Distribution Service

When distributing press releases on your own you save the money it would cost to have a service do it. You can also be more targeted in your efforts than a service would. Some services' lists may be outdated or incomplete. Their lists of reporters and editors may not be comprehensive and may not have been updated.

On the other hand, some services may get your press release taken more seriously. If the reporter recognizes the name of the service they may be more receptive than if it were to come from an unknown company. Using a service is bound to save you a lot of time.

If you decide to send your press releases on your own, you will have to build a list of journalists. When reading publications, look for the names of reporters and find out their contact information. If you don't know who to send a press release to at any publication you can always call and ask for the name of the appropriate editor.

Subscribe to a personalized news service to receive articles about your industry. This is a great way to find the names of journalists who might be interested in what you have to say.

There are a number of online resources to assist you in building your press distribution list, such as the one shown in Figure 14.2. Mediafinder (*http://www.mediafinder.com*) is a web site that may be useful. It provides access to a database of thousands of media outlets including magazines, journals, newspapers, newsletters, and catalogs.

There are a number of press release distribution services online. You will find a number of them in the Internet Resources at the end of this chapter.

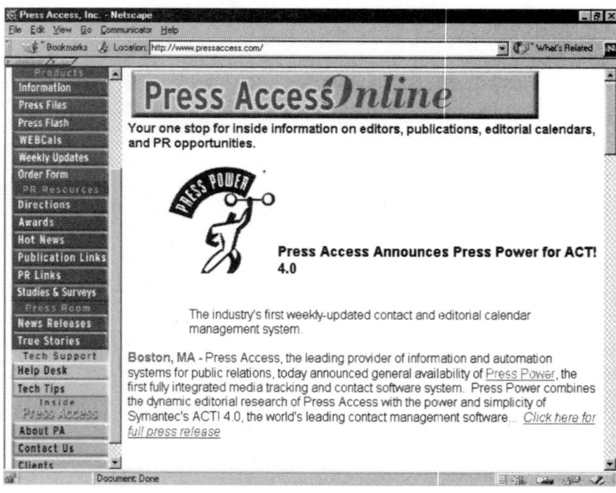

Figure 14.2. Press Access Online provides information on editorial calendars and editors and their preferences.

Golden Tips for Press Release Distribution

When distributing your press releases don't send them to the news desk unaddressed. Know which editor handles the type of news in your release and address the press release to that person. Don't send the press release to more than one editor in any organization unless there is more than one angle to the information in the press release.

Call ahead, if possible, to discuss and solicit the editor's interest in your press release before sending it. Also, follow up with a phone call a few days later to ensure it was received and to answer any questions.

Press Release Timing and Deadlines

One of the most important things to remember when sending a press release or advisory is the deadline. Know how far in advance you should send your information for each of the different media. Here are some time guidelines for your press release distribution.

Monthly Magazines

For monthly magazines you should submit your press releases at least two to three months before the issue you want it to appear in. Magazines are planned far in advance because it often takes a number of weeks to have the magazine printed and in subscriber's mailboxes.

Daily Newspapers

It is a good idea to have your press release arrive on the editor's desk at least several weeks in advance. If it concerns a special holiday, you should send it even earlier.

TV and Radio

When submitting press releases to TV and radio, remember that you may be asked to appear on a show as a guest. Be prepared for this before you submit the release. TV and radio move very quickly; a story that has been given to the news director in the morning may appear on that evening's news.

Formatting Your E-mail Press Release

You press releases can be e-mailed. Some reporters prefer e-mailed releases while others say they prefer mailed or faxed releases. Check the reporter's preference before you send your press release. If you send e-mailed press releases, make sure that your e-mails are formatted properly. Refer to Chapter 5 for guidelines on how to create effective e-mail messages.

Keep your e-mailed press releases to one or two pages with short paragraphs. It is best to include the press release inserted in the e-mail. Do not send your press release as an attachment. You don't know which platform or word processing program the reporter is using. There may also be problems downloading, which may prevent your release from being read.

Make sure the subject line of your e-mail is compelling. E-mailed releases can be easily deleted, unopened, by the journalist. Make sure your e-mail is clear and concise. Get to the point with the first sentence. If you don't grab the reader's attention at the beginning of the release the recipient may not keep reading to find out what your news is.

What Is Considered Newsworthy?

Your press release has to contain newsworthy information for it to be published. One of the main concerns for public relations representatives is figuring out what is considered newsworthy and what isn't. You have to have a catch, and, if possible, it should appeal to some sort of emotion. Below is a list of newsworthy items:

- A merger or partnership between your company and another

- A free service or resource offered by your company to the general public
- A survey or forum discussing an already hot news topic being held by your company
- The appearance of a celebrity at a company event
- The findings of a report your company has conducted
- A breakthrough in technology resulting in a significant new consumer product
- A charity contribution by your company
- A milestone anniversary that your company is celebrating
- An award presented by your company

What Isn't Considered Newsworthy?

Some things that aren't news to the general public may be news to targeted trade magazines and journals. Use your own judgment when trying to determine if your press release is news or just an excuse to get your company's name in the press. If your release focuses on any of the following, it is probably not newsworthy enough to publish.

The launch of a new web site has not been news for a number of years now. Unless the site is based on a breakthrough in Internet technology or serves the public interest in an innovative way, you won't get a mention in the news. Nor is a new feature or change to your web site newsworthy information. Even if your site has undergone a major overhaul, this is not news to the general public.

Launching a new product is not newsworthy unless the product represents a significant breakthrough in some area. The upgrade of an old product simply won't cut it.

Preparing Your Press Kits/Media Kits

Your press kit is an essential item at press conferences and interviews. This kit can also be sent to reporters when they request more information about a press release you have sent to them.

Your press kit should start with a folder displaying your company logo and basic contact information. The folder should have pockets inside so that different sheets of information can be inserted. The following items should be included in your press kit:

- A press release outlining the newsworthy event
- A company history
- Brochures
- Other articles written about your company
- Pictures
- Background information on key players
- FAQ answers to anticipated questions
- Quotes from key individuals
- Contact information
- Business card

Develop an Online Media Center for Public Relations

If publicity is a significant part of your public relations strategy you should consider developing an online media center as part of your site (Figures 14.3 and 14.4). The Media Center would have all the components of a press kit with interlinking components. The Media Center should provide everything a journalist or editor might look for when writing an article on your business.

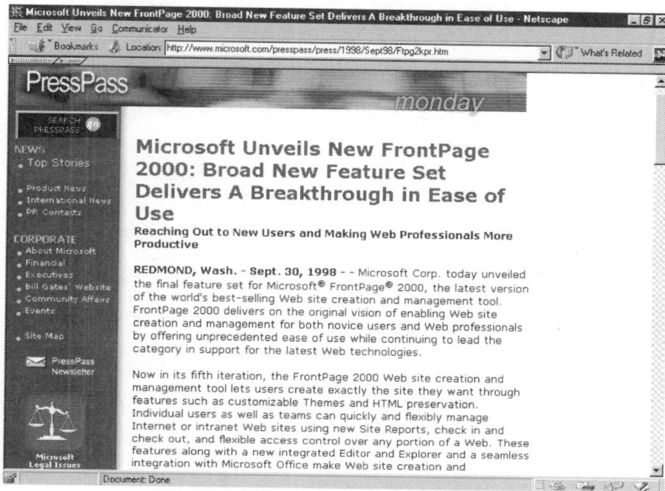

Figure 14.3. Microsoft's Media Center - PressPass makes information readily available to the press.

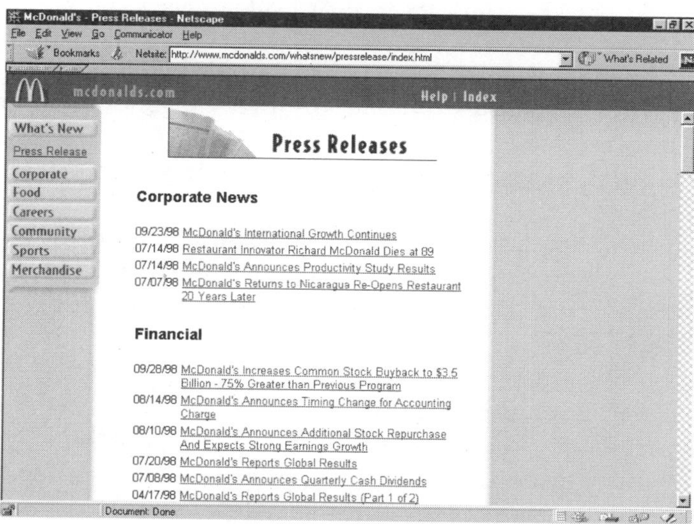

Figure 14.4. McDonald's provides an archive of their press releases online.

Internet Resources for Chapter 14

Press Releases

Press Release Tips for PR People
http://marketing.tenagra.com/releases.html
Talks about what one expects to receive and how you should write releases.

Executive Summary: Understanding News
http://www.x-summary.com/tips/052698.html
Improve the reception of your press releases by knowing what is news and what isn't.

PR Tips
http://www.profilepr.co.uk/prforum/PRTIPS/PRTIPS6.HTM
A British agency reviews the pros and cons of e-mail press releases.

Care & Feeding of the Press
http://www.netpress.org/careandfeeding.html
Journalist's manifesto for how PR people should work with the media.

The Press Release Recycle Bin's Always Full
http://www.anvil-media.com/archivenew/0598mmedia/column/pressrelease.html
A brief, but good, list of press release tips to help you succeed.

Journalists aren't the only ones reading your press releases
http://www.ragan.com/newsletter/Article_IPR_3749.html
How online press releases reach audiences that extend well beyond journalists.

Don't Drop the PR Ball
http://www.searchz.com/wmo/dontdroppr.shtml
A brief example of how a PR pro blew it with a reporter.

A Template for a Killer Press Release
http://www.netrageousresults.com/pr/prtemplate.html
Example format for a successful press release to get yours noticed.

Where to Submit Your Press Releases

E-mail Press Release Service Comparison
http://www.urlwire.com/email-releases.html
A decent comparison between different e-mail press release services. Caution: the author owns the first one listed.

Multimedia Marketing Group
http://www.mmgco.com/
WebStep: a web site promotion service and list of self-help resources.

Partyline
http://www.partylinepublishing.com
The standard media placement newsletter for the public relations trade.

PR Newswire Home Page
http://www.prnewswire.com
A leading source for worldwide corporate media, business, the financial community, and the individual investor.

Internet News Bureau Press Release Service
http://www.newsbureau.com
For a fee you can distribute your press release to thousands of online media outlets here. Also links to a number of good PR resources.

Promote Mailing Lists and Newsletters

Tell Liszt about Lists
http://www.liszt.com/submit.html
Register your mailing list with a major online database to get yourself noticed.

NewJour Welcome page
http://gort.ucsd.edu/newjour/NewJourWel.html
Home for many Internet newsletters.

The List Exchange
http://www.listex.com
Directory of mailing lists and resources for those who run them.

Paid Help

Internet Media Fax
http://www.imediafax.com
Custom online news distribution service that creates targeted media lists "on the fly."

Internet Wire
http://www.internetwire.com
The Internet Wire offers online press release distribution via e-mail.

Xpress Press News Release Distribution Service
http://www.xpresspress.com
Press releases delivered electronically by Email to 4000 journalists and media members in the U.S. and internationally.

PressLine Data Base for Press Releases
http://pressline.com
Press release database organized by industry, available in English, German, and French.

Tracing the Ownership of Online News
http://olj.usc.edu/sections/news/98_stories/ojrnews_corpownership_tracing.htm
Summary of business interests for ten of the top business and technology online news publishers.

Tips for Printed Press Releases

14 Tips for Sending Effective Press Releases
http://www.azstarnet.com:80/~poewar/writer/press.html
Tips to get the best results with press releases.

15

Online Publications

Ezines
Electronic magazines

More than 60 percent of Internet users frequently read online publications. Identify appropriate marketing opportunities by searching for and reading ezines that are relevant to your business. In this chapter we will cover:

- What are electronic magazines?
- Finding online sites to advertise or arrange links
- How to find appropriate ezines for marketing purposes
- Submitting articles to appropriate ezines
- Advertising in appropriate ezines
- Ezine resources online

Appealing to Magazine Subscribers on the Net

A recent NPD Online Research survey shows that six out of ten web users frequently read online publications or "**ezines.**" This is one of the reasons they are among the most popular marketing tools on the Internet. Five years ago there were a few hundred ezines in publication. Now there are thousands of ezines dedicated to a wide variety of topics such as travel, business opportunities, food, child care—you name it. For any topic you are interested in, there are quite likely several ezines dedicated to it.

What Exactly Are Ezines?

Ezines are the online version of magazines. They contain information regarding a certain topic in the form of magazine articles and features. Some ezines are web site based and others are e-mail based.

Many offline magazines provide a version online as well (Figure 15.1). *Time, People* and *Sports Illustrated* all are accessible via the Internet. There are other web based ezines that have only an online presence. (Figure 15.2)

These ezines are accessed through their web sites. Usually there is no charge to view the web based ezines but some do charge a subscription fee.

These web-based ezines tend to be as graphically pleasing as offline magazines.

E-mail Ezines

E-mail ezines are not nearly as pretty as the web based ezines. They tend to be more content oriented and, as such, tend to be more of a target marketing mechanism. E-mail ezines tend to be several pages in length with several articles and often have classified advertising. Circulation of these ezines is often in the thousands. Most of these ezines run weekly or bi-weekly editions.

Interested individuals subscribe and the ezine is delivered straight into their e-mail boxes. Those individuals that are interested in the

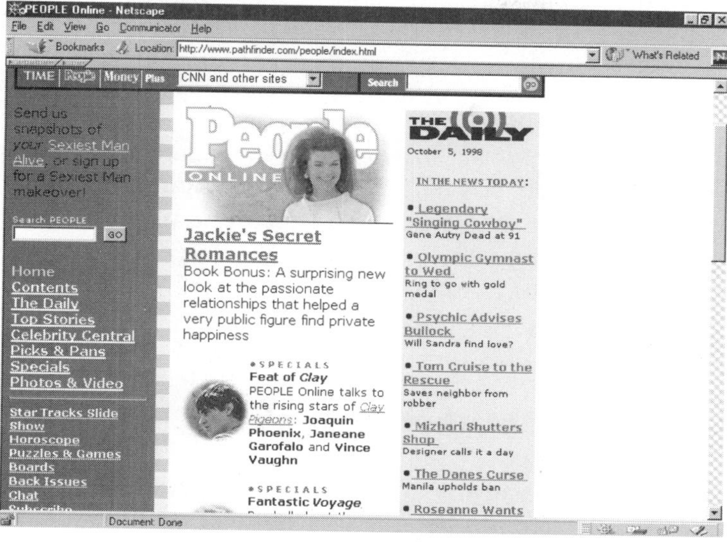

Figure 15.1. *People Magazine* is an example of an offline magazine that has an online version.

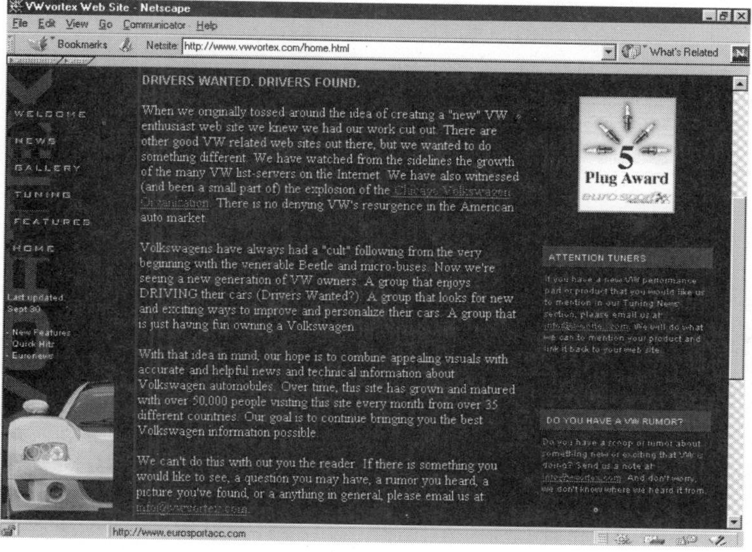

Figure 15.2. VW Vortex is an example of a web-based ezine.

subject have taken the time to subscribe, and ask to receive the information directly in their e-mail box. Once you have found an ezine that caters to your target market, the ezine may be a very valuable marketing vehicle.

Every subscriber to an e-mail based ezine has access to the Internet. They regularly receive and send e-mail and quite likely surf the Net. If you advertise in this type of medium and place your Internet address in the ad, your prospective customer is not more than a couple of clicks away from your site.

Using Ezines as Marketing Tools

Online publications are superior marketing tools for a number of reasons. They can be used in a number of different ways to increase the traffic to your web site. You can:

- Advertise directly
- Be a sponsor
- Submit articles
- Send press releases
- Start your own

Finding Appropriate Ezines for Your Marketing Effort

There are many locations online to find lists and links to both web based and e-mail ezines. A number of these resources are listed in the Internet Resources at the end of this chapter.

The most important element of choosing an ezine is to choose one that reaches your target market. The reason ezine ads are effective is that there is a high correlation between the target customer and the magazine's subscribers. If you advertise in an ezine simply because it has the largest subscriber rate, you will probably be disappointed unless your products or services have mass market appeal.

You should review a number of the ezine-listing sites, like the one shown in Figure 15.3. Some of these sites have search capabilities on appropriate keywords. Others have their ezines listed by category. Once you have a list of ezines you feel fit well with your marketing objectives, you should subscribe and begin receiving and reviewing these ezines.

The Multiple Advantages of Ezine Advertising

One of the major advantages of ezine advertising is the life span of your ads. Ezines that are delivered to e-mail addresses will be read by

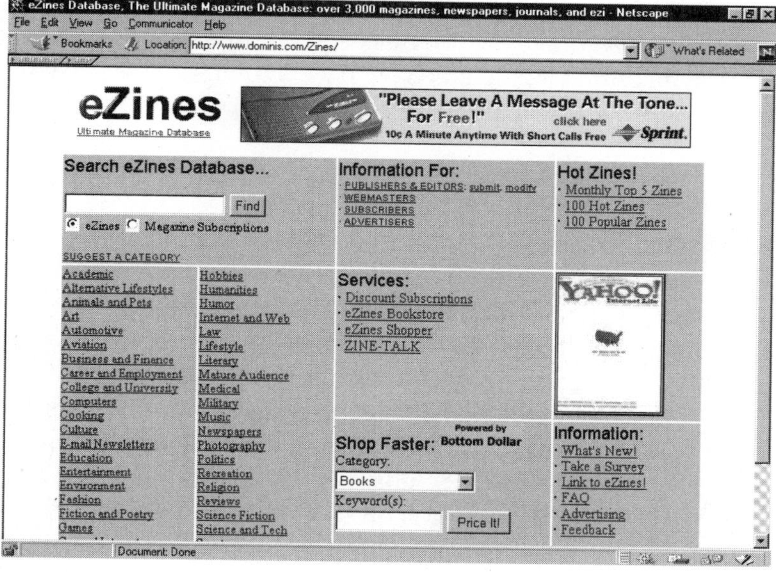

Figure 15.3. The Ultimate Magazine Database provided by Dominis provides a searchable directory of over 3,000 magazines, newspapers, journals, and ezines.

the recipient and sometimes saved for future reference. Many ezines archive their issues with the ads intact. Advertisers have received responses to ads that are several months old! Keep in mind, the immediate results of this advertising method will not be as impressive as a banner ad displayed for a limited time.

Another advantage of ezine advertising is that ezines are often shared with friends and associates. Your ad may be passed around a number of times after it first entered the mailbox of the subscriber. You are being charged for the ad based on the number of e-mail subscribers. Therefore, the extra viewers of your ad will be at no cost to you.

One of the most tangible advantages of ezine advertising is the relatively low cost. Ezines need to fill all of their available space. If an ezine advertising section has empty spaces, they are often willing to negotiate. Some will even barter with you, advertising space at a discounted price in exchange for their ezine promotion on your web site.

Ezines provide a very targeted advertising medium. People subscribe to various ezines because they have a genuine interest in the topics covered. This provides a major advantage over other advertising mediums. Ezine ads have been shown to have very high response rates due to their targeted nature.

Guidelines for your Advertising

Once you have found ezines that reach your target market, you should consider a number of other factors before you place your ad.

- Check the ads displayed in the ezine for repetition. If advertisers have not advertised more than once, then they probably did not see very positive results.

- Respond to some of the ads and ask the advertiser what their experiences were with advertising in that particular ezine. Be sure to tell them who you are and why you are contacting them. If you are up front, they will probably be receptive to your inquiry.

- Talk to the ezine publisher and ask questions; for instance, how many subscribers there are. Ask what other advertisers have had to say about their results. Find out what types of ads they accept and if there are any restrictions. Maybe the ezine has a set of advertising policies that you can receive via E-mail.

- Find out if your ad can have a hypertext link to your web site. If the ezine allows hypertext links make sure you link to an appropriate page, one which is a continuation of the advertisement or a page that provides details on the item you were advertising. Provide a link to the order form from this page to assist the transaction.

- In some cases the ezine will have an editorial calendar available to assist you with the timing of your ad. The editorial calendar will tell you what articles will be included in upcoming issues. If an upcoming issue will have an article relating to your type of products or services you may choose to advertise in that issue. You might contact the editor regarding a product review or submit an article relevant to the issue topics.

- Make sure that the advertising rates are reasonable based on the number of subscribers, and ask yourself if you can afford it. If you are not in a position to pay for the advertising now, ask if there are any other arrangements that could be made. For example, the publisher may accept a link on your web site in exchange for the ad.

- You should develop your ads with your target customer in mind. They should attract your best prospects. Wherever possible you should link to your site or provide an e-mail link to the appropriate individual within your organization.

- You should develop a mechanism to track advertising responses. You could use different e-mail accounts for different ads to determine which ads are bringing you the responses. You can also use different URLs to point the viewer to different pages within your site. If you have a good traffic analysis package you will be able to track the increase in visitors as a result of your ad.

- Make sure you are versed in the publication's advertising deadlines and ad format preferences.

Other Marketing Opportunities with Ezines

Besides advertising there are a number of other marketing opportunities that can be explored with ezines (Figure 15.4).

Once you have found the ezines that cater to your target market these ezines may be appropriate recipients for your press releases.

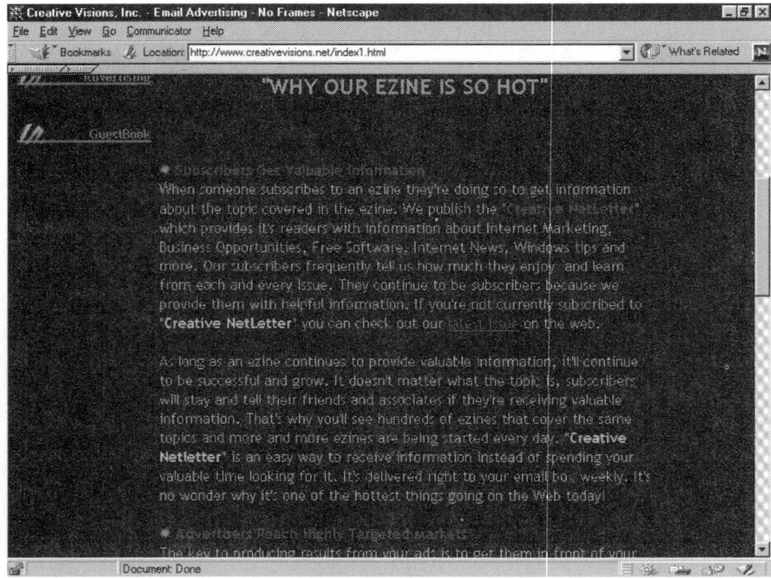

Figure 15.4. Creative Visions provides an e-mail-based ezine called *Creative Newsletter*, which covers a range of topics including Internet marketing.

Refer to Chapter 14 for recommendations on press release development and distribution.

The editors may also accept articles of interest to their readership. You might be able to incorporate information on your products and services in an interesting article that would fit the editor's guidelines.

Starting Your Own Ezine

You can start you own ezine. Don't make this decision without lots of thought. There are lots of resources online regarding ezine development and administration.

Internet Resources for Chapter 15

John Labovitz's E-Zine-List
http://www.meer.net/~johnl/ezine-list
This is a list of electronic ezines around the world, accessible via the Web, FTP, e-mail, and other services. The list is updated approximately monthly and contains 2,431 ezines.

Factsheet Five
http://www.factsheet5.com
A site dedicated to ezines. How to's, reviews, FAQs, and a list of ezines on the Internet. This is a selection of favorite web sites.

The Etext Archives
http://www.etext.org/Zines
Complete with a search engine, this site offers places to find all of your online publication resources.

Electronic Newsstand
http://www.enews.com
Founded in 1993, this was one of the first content-based sites on the Internet. Since then, the site has grown to become the largest and most diverse magazine-related resource anywhere on the web.

MediaFinder
http://www.mediafinder.com/magazines/mag0020.cfm
A national directory of magazines with details on target audience, publisher, contact, telephone numbers, web addresses, e-mail addresses, editorial descriptions, issue frequency, and subscription price. In a lot of cases there is an Information Request form attached should you want further details. Great resource!

WebPlaces
http://www.webplaces.com/ezines.htm
A meta-index of ezines sorted by category.

Ecola Newsstand
http://www.ecola.com
Ecola's Newsstand has over 6,800 magazines, newspapers, and publications. There are over 100 categories of magazines to choose from.

Ezine Search
http://www.homeincome.com/search-it/ezine
Billed as the world's ultimate e-magazine database. Searchable by category.

Ezines Ultimate Magazine Database
http://www.dominis.com/Zines
Another huge database of ezines searchable by category.

LinkPad-Electronic Magazines
http://www.referthem.com/pad/ezines.htm
A list of Electronic Magazines and directories.

16

Web Rings As a Promotion Tool

Web Ring
A ring of linked Internet sites

Web rings provide a different way to organize sites. They are a free service offered to the Internet Community. **Web rings** arrange sites with similar content by linking them together in a circle, or a ring. Each link in the ring is directed to a CGI script on the web ring's server which sends the viewer on to the next site in the ring. There are literally thousands of rings with subjects like communications, games, art, real estate, etc. If there isn't a ring suitable for your site, you can create your own. The types of visitors you will receive from participating in the web ring will be potential customers who are responsive to the content of your site and curious about your products or services. In this chapter we cover:

- What are web rings and how do they work?
- Promotion possibilities with web rings
- How do I participate and what will it cost?
- Where to find web rings that work for your company
- Web ring resources on the Net

An Effective Alternative to Search Engines and Directories

Web rings are a fast-growing service on the Internet, providing one of the easiest ways for visitors to navigate the Internet. In each of its tens of thousands of topic-specific rings, member web sites have linked their sites together, thus permitting more targeted visitors to reach the joined sites quickly and easily.

People have been becoming increasingly dissatisfied with search engines and directories as tools to identify specific topic-related sites. Searches on a specific keyword have yielded results that often include totally unrelated sites. The web ring provides an alternative to these tools.

Site owners typically "trade links" with other web sites to help advertise each other's sites. The web ring was initially developed to enlarge the scope of link trading. A web ring joins together many sites with a common topic.

Two of the major web ring sites are:

- WebRing at *http://www.webring.org*
- LoopLink at *http://www.looplink.com*

What are Web Rings?

A web ring is made up of a number of topic-specific sites that are grouped together, as shown in Figure 16.1. There are Titanic web rings, Beanie Baby web rings, prenatal care web rings, BMW web rings, and remote sensing web rings in the list of over 40,000 web rings that exist today. At *webring.org,* web rings fit into several major categories:

- Arts and Humanities
- Computers
- Business and Economy

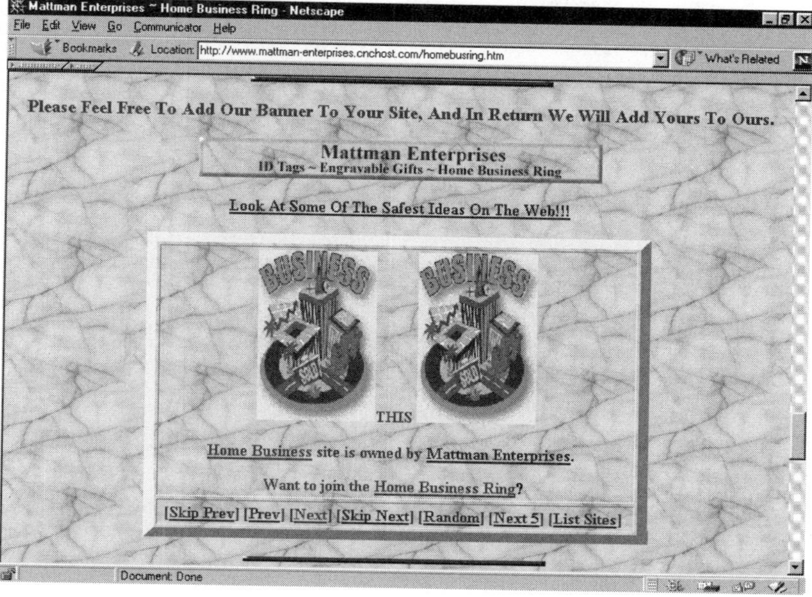

Figure 16.1. The Home Business Ring displays the common web ring graphic at the bottom of the page. The navigation tool allows you to travel easily throughout the ring.

- Internet
- Health
- Recreation and Sports
- Entertainment
- Society and Culture
- Miscellaneous

Each of these major categories has a number of subcategories, and each of the subcategories has a number of individual rings.

Rings can contain any number of sites. There must be at least five before the ring will be listed in the directories. Generally, the rings will contain somewhere between 20 and 200 sites. Some rings are smaller and some rings are substantially higher with close to a thousand sites included.

Each ring was started and is maintained by an individual web site owner. Through navigation links found most often at the bottom of member pages, visitors can travel to all or any of the sites in a ring. They can move through a ring in either direction, going to the next or previous site, or listing the next five sites in the ring. Visitors can also jump to a random site in the ring, or survey all the sites that make up the ring.

An extraordinary system, web rings are entirely open and free of charge to both visitors and members. As more and more people discover web rings, we will see phenomenal growth in this as a preferred method to surf the net. Today web rings are experiencing growth rates in excess of 10% monthly. Member sites total over 500,000 and web rings total over 40,000.

How Do Web Rings Work?

To surf a ring, all you have to do is use the links at the bottom of the page in the "web ring block." At the bottom of web ring participant's pages, you will find the web ring navigation aid. A common web ring graphic will include links to the "next" site in the ring, the "previous" site in the ring, or a "random" site in the ring. You also have the option, in many cases, to see a list of the "next 5" sites in the ring or to view the entire "index" of the ring's sites. Once you begin surfing a ring, there is no clear beginning or ending, just a circle of related material.

The web ring program compensates for sites that are unreachable because they no longer exist or have server problems. You will always be able to navigate the loop.

When using a search engine you are provided with a list of resulting sites, only some of which are appropriate. You visit the sites listed and then, depending on which browser you are using, you may use your "back" button to return to the results page to make another selection. With a web ring this backing out is unnecessary. Once you're finished reviewing a site in the ring you proceed to the next site that is of interest or simply surf through the connected sites one by one.

How to Participate in Web Rings

The first thing to do is find web rings that are appropriate for your product or service, those that cater to your target market. You can review the directories at the WebRing site *http://www.webring.org* and also at the LoopLink site *http://www.looplink.com.*

Once you have found an appropriate web ring you contact the owner to ask permission to join. The owner will review your site to determine your "fit" with the theme. Once you are accepted the owner will provide you with the required bit of code (and accompanying graphics), which you will insert on your page. The ring owner provides all the required material, you slip it into your HTML file, and that's that.

Once the code is on your site, *webring.org* monitors the traffic and collects the stats for your site as they do for all web ring sites.

Any web site owner can apply to create a new ring if they feel none already existing suit their needs. If the application is approved, *webring.org* will provide all the necessary code and instructions. New web rings are listed in the directory once they contain at least five sites.

Web Ring Participation Costs

The cost to participate in these web rings is absolutely nil. No application fees, no charge for the approval, no charge for the code to be inserted on your pages, no charge for the increased traffic a web ring brings.

The Benefits of Web Rings

There are many benefits to both the users of web rings and the participating web sites. Benefits to the user include:

- Web rings provide a great navigation tool when looking for more information on a specific topic.

- Web rings are easy to use. The provide one of the most efficient ways to find specific content on the Internet.

- Web rings avoid the duplication found in search engines where a site may appear several times in one search. Each site is linked only once in each web ring.
- Web rings speed up search time.
- Web rings eliminate sifting through mounds of search engine results for appropriate sites.

Benefits to participating web sites include:

- Web ring participation increases the number of targeted visitors to your web site.
- The organizers of the web rings make it easy to monitor how successful your ring is. Traffic reports and "top" rings statistics are made available to participants.
- Web rings drive traffic to your site.

Business Reluctance to Participate in Web Rings

One of the biggest hurdles web rings face to being adopted by the business sector is that when you join a ring, you are linking to the competition, as shown in Figure 16.2.

It is likely this mentality explains why rings have been so popular for personal sites and special interest groups, but have failed to catch on in today's business. But, again, small businesses and retail-oriented sites have not shied away from rings. For example, rings and banner programs are hot marketing strategies for stores that sell collectibles. This is particularly true for hard-to-find collectibles. Take the Beanie Babies phenomenon: *Not* being on a Beanie web ring or participating in Beanie-specific banner programs, could be a crucial mistake for vendors. After all, if a customer hits a site and they don't have a specific "Beanie," the quest isn't over—it's on to the next site. And what better way to get there than via a ring. Your site might just be the next one.

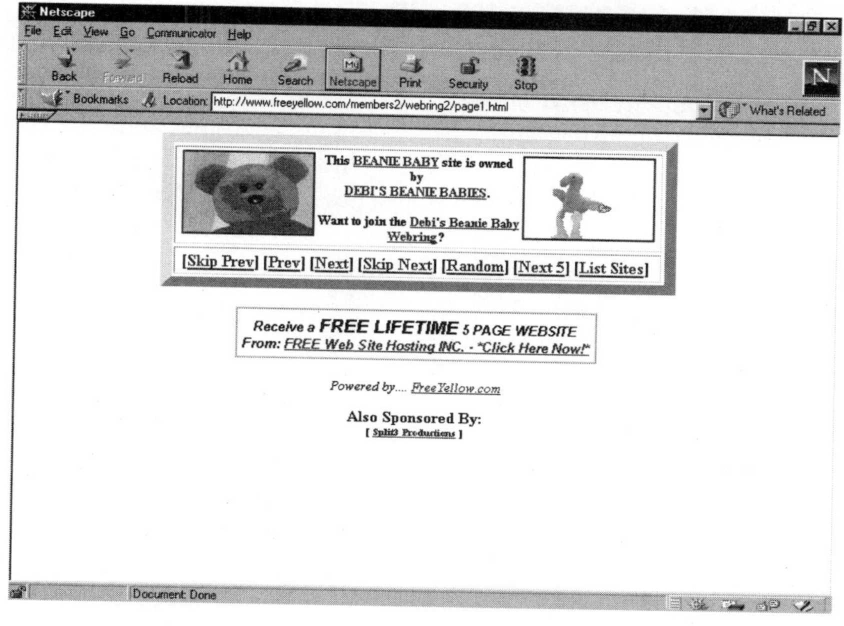

Figure 16.2. The Beanie Baby Webring is an example of a ring that contains many competing businesses.

Other Marketing Opportunities Provided by Web Rings

When you have found a web ring that attracts your target market you can participate and enjoy the increase in visitors to your site. Web rings provide an array of other opportunities as well.

You can search through the list of participants in a web ring to arrange reciprocal links. You can also search a web ring for banner advertising purposes. You can either exchange banners or purchase advertising on these sites.

You can find sites that may be appropriate for co-operative advertising purposes. You can exchange coupons with another site you are linked to, which works especially well when you sell non-competing products to the same target market.

Internet Resources for Chapter 16

Web ring - The Shape of Things to Come
http://www.webring.org
One of the fastest and most exciting ways to navigate the World Wide Web. In each of its tens of thousands of rings, member web sites have banded together to form their sites into linked circles. Their purpose is to allow more visitors to reach them quickly and easily.

LoopLink - The Traffic Building Site
http://www.looplink.com
Sites of a particular subject together in a loop. A visitor to any loop site can easily move forward or backward through the loop and visit other loop sites within that subject area. This drives targeted qualified traffic to all the loop sites. Surfers don't want to deal with mounds of irrelevant search engine results. They want to visit sites on topics they love. It's so simple, and everybody's a winner.

RingSurf
http://www.ringsurf.com
RingSurf is a completely free service that lets user quickly, easily, and reliably navigate thousands of related web sites organized by areas of interest. Joining a Net Ring is great way to increase traffic to your site.

17

Effective Offline Promotion

There are many benefits to cross-promoting your web site using traditional media and print materials. Your web site can answer a lot of questions and provide more information than you can print in a magazine or newspaper ad. Your site can be kept up to date with the latest information available. People can request additional information or order online. In this chapter we cover:

- Tips for offline promotion of your web site
- Offline promotion opportunities

Offline Promotion Objectives

Since visitors can be directed from offline promotion to request additional information or order online, you should promote your URL on every piece of promotional material you produce! The more exposure your URL receives the more likely people will remember it when they go online.

Be creative with your offline promotion campaign. Brainstorm with innovative thinkers to come up with a number of good places to promote your URL; for example, try displaying your URL in your TV and radio commercials, magazine and newspaper ads, and billboards. The more places your URL appears, the more it will get noticed. Some businesses even incorporate their URL into their building signage.

By displaying your URL in traditional media, people are encouraged to visit your site for more information about your company. Another benefit is that people can usually order from your web site. Naturally, your site should be up to date with all of the latest information on products, prices, and sales promotions. If a six-month old advertisement is seen in a magazine, as long as the URL is displayed in the ad, readers can go to your site and get current information. Your web site is your most effective advertisement, but it is an advertisement that people have to know about before they can view it.

URL Exposure Through Corporate Literature and Material

It is important to maintain a consistent corporate image in both your online and offline promotional campaigns. Businesses should use the same logo and/or tag lines on all of their marketing materials. As a rule of thumb, try to place your URL on everything you put your logo on—which means just about every piece of corporate literature.

For example:

- Letterhead
- Business cards
- Corporate brochures
- Envelopes
- Checks
- Fax coversheets
- Report covers

- Flyers
- Advertisements
- Direct mail pieces
- Newsletters
- Press releases
- Mediakits

URL Exposure Through Promotional Items

If your company uses promotional items as give-aways at trade shows and events it is a good idea to incorporate your web site marketing with these items. Items that are used in and around computer work-stations are ideal because your URL is visible when people are in a position to actually visit your site. Some examples are:

- Mouse pads
- Diskette holders
- Screen cleaning kits
- Software
- Screen savers
- Pens and pencils
- Scratch pads
- Coffee mugs
- Coasters

- Letter openers
- Stress balls
- Calendars
- Sticky notes

URL Exposure Through Clothing

Articles of clothing are another great promotional item. When someone wears an article of clothing with your URL on it, they become a walking billboard for your site. If you have a corporate uniform, your URL could be displayed. Put your URL and a catchy phrase or tag line on items such as:

- Golf shirts
- T-shirts
- Sweatshirts
- Hats
- Aprons
- Jackets

URL Exposure on Novelty Items

Novelty items can be an effective place to print your URL. If your target market is a younger audience, then put your URL on items that will appeal to them, such as:

- Frisbees

- Balls
- Beach towels
- Sunglasses
- Key chains
- Magnets
- Chocolate bars
- Lighters and matches
- Bumper stickers

Promotion with a Touch of Creativity

Be creative and come up with catchy slogans that have a connection with the promotional item. For example:

- **Clocks:** "Take some time to visit our web site at..."
- **Rulers:** "For a measurable difference visit us at..."
- **Coffee mugs:** "Take a coffee break and visit our web site at..."
- **Tape measures:** "Visit our web site at *http://www.YourURL.com* and see if our site measures up."
- **Magnifying glasses:** "You don't need one of these to see that our site is the best. Come visit us online at..."
- **Watches:** "Isn't it about time you visited us at..."
- **Bookmarks:** "Take a break from reading and visit our web site at..."

Special Holidays

Use holidays to promote your site by giving away items that will likely be circulated; for example, gift tags and bags, greeting cards.

URL Exposure on Your Products

If possible, put your URL on your products themselves. This is an innovative idea that Joe Boxer has implemented. They stitch their URL into the waistband of their underwear.

Internet Resources for Chapter 17

AdResource
http://www.adresource.com/html/body_web_marketing.html
Ad Resource specializes in web marketing and promotion resources, articles, and consulting services as well as web marketing software development.

Promotional Webstickers
http://www.websticker.com/products.htm
Simple ideas to effectively promote your web site offline.

MediaFinder
http://www.wprc.com/wpl/offline.html
Articles on promoting your web site offline.

Bizine
http://www.bizine.com/profit.htm
Increase your profits by coordinating online and traditional offline marketing. An article by Bob LeDuc.

Appendix A

Terminology

ASCII Text File (American Standard Code for Information Interchange) The worldwide standard format for text files in computers and on the Internet. The code represents all the uppercase and lowercase letters, numbers, punctuation, etc. There are 128 standard ASCII codes in which a 7-digit binary number, 0000000 through 1111111, represents each character.

Backbone Large transmission lines that carry data being transferred from smaller lines. These lines or paths connect local or regional networks together for long-distance communication. The connection points are known as network nodes or telecommunication data switching exchanges (DSEs).

BBS - Bulletin Board System A computer that can be reached by computer modem dialing (or by Telnet) for the purpose of sharing or exchanging messages or other files. Some BBSs are devoted to specific interests; others offer a more general service. The definitive BBS List says that there are over 40,000 BBSs worldwide.

Benchmark A point of reference by which something can be measured or compared. In surveying, a "bench mark" (two words) is a post or other permanent mark used as the basis for measuring the elevation of other topographical points.

Browser The software used to view the various kinds of Internet resources, or sites.

Cache A place to store something more or less temporarily. Web pages you request are stored in your browser's cache (pronounced "cash") directory on your hard disk. When you return to a page you've recently looked at, the browser can get most of the information from the cache rather than the original server. A cache saves you time and the network the burden of some additional traffic. You can usually vary the size of your cache, depending on your particular browser.

CGI - Common Gateway Interface Guidelines that define how a web server communicates with another piece of software on the same machine, and how the other piece of software, the CGI program, talks to the web server. Any piece of software can be a CGI program if it handles input and output according to the CGI standard.

Cgi-bin This is the most common name for the directory on a web server that holds a CGI program. Most programs located in the cgi-bin directory are text files, scripts that are executed by binaries located elsewhere on the same machine.

Cookie On the Internet, a cookie refers to a piece of information sent by a web server to a web browser. The browser software is expected to save the cookie and send the information back to the server whenever an additional request is made. Cookies may contain information such as user preferences, registration or login information, online shopping cart info, etc.

Crawlers Crawlers quietly comb through websites and index the information they find.

CPM - Cost Per Thousand Page Views This is a measure taken from print advertising. Since not all page views result in seeing the ad (for example, if a page scrolls, an ad may be initially out of view), CPM is often interpreted to mean the cost per thousand ad views. (The "M" is the Roman numeral M.) CPTM Cost per thousand targeted ad views. This implies that the audience you have targeted is of a particular demographic. (See "Demographics" below.)

Cybernaut A person who uses the Internet.

Cyberspace Used to describe all areas of information resources available through computer networks and the Internet. William Gibson originated the term in his novel *Neuromancer.*

Demographics Specific data about the size and characteristics of a population or audience that can be used for marketing purposes.

Domain Name The unique name that identifies an Internet site. A domain name always has two or more parts, separated by dots. The part on the left is the most specific, and the part on the right is the most general. A given machine may have more than one domain name but a given domain name points to only one machine. For example, the domain names: *everyopportunity.com* and *support.everyopportunity.com* can all refer to the same machine.

E-mail - Electronic Mail **Mail** messages, usually text, sent from one person to another via computer. Messages can also be sent automatically to a large number of addresses on a mailing list.

Ezine, e-Zine - Electronic Magazine Used to describe an electronic magazine, including those of print magazines such as *National Geographic* and *Newsweek* that have electronic editions. Thus, E-Zine Database includes both electronic-only magazines together with electronic-edition magazines.

FAQs – Frequently Asked Questions Documents that list and answer the most common questions on a particular subject or problem area. There are hundreds of FAQs on subjects as diverse as car repair and franchise advice.

Firewall A set of related programs located at a network gateway server to protect the resources of a private network from users of other networks.

Flame, Flaming Flaming usually involves the use of harsh language directed towards a group or individual for sending unwanted messages (marketing) on a newsgroup or mail list.

Forums Another name for a newsgroup in which people are formed together in a group to chat and discuss.

FTP - File Transfer Protocol The common method of moving files between two computers through the Internet medium. FTP is a special way to login to another computer or Internet site for the purposes of retrieving and/or sending files.

Hit A single request from a web browser for a single item from a web server; thus in order for a web browser to display a page that contains three graphics, four "hits" would occur at the server: one for the HTML page, and one for each of the three graphics. Hits are often used as a rough measure of visits on a server.

Home Page, Homepage The main web page for a business, organization, person—or simply the main page of a collection of web pages.

Host Any computer on a network that can hold files available to other computers on the network. It is quite common to have one host machine provide several services to other machines, such as WWW and Usenet.

HTML - HyperText Markup Language, HTM The coding language used to create documents for use on the World Wide Web. These documents have a file extension of html or htm. HTML code looks a lot like old-fashioned typesetting code, where you surround a block of text with codes that indicate how it should appear. HTML or HTM files are meant to be viewed using a World Wide Web client program, such as Netscape or Internet Explorer.

HTTP - HyperText Transport Protocol The most important protocol used in the World Wide Web for moving hypertext files across the Internet. Requires an HTTP client program on one end, and an HTTP server program on the other end.

Hypertext Clickable text that links to another document; that is, words or phrases in one document that can be clicked on by a reader, causing another document to be retrieved and displayed.

Image Map A single graphic that has multiple hot links to different pages or resources.

Intranet A private network inside a company or organization that uses the same kinds of software found on the public Internet, but that is only for internal use and cannot be viewed outside the network.

ISDN - Integrated Services Digital Network A quicker way to move more data over existing regular phone lines. Rapidly becoming available around the world, it is priced comparably to standard analog phone circuits. It can provide speeds of roughly 128,000 bits-per-second over the regular phone lines.

ISP - Internet Service Provider A provider that allows access to the Internet. Usually there is a cost to the consumer, although there are still some free community networks. Java Programming language that is specifically designed for writing programs. It can be safely downloaded to your computer through the

Internet and immediately run without fear of viruses or other harm to your computer. Using small Java programs, called "Applets," web pages can include functions such as animations, calculators, and other fancy tricks that cannot be done by normal HTML.

LAN - Local Area Network A network limited to the local area, usually the same building or floor of a company.

Login The account name used to gain access to a computer system, not a password. Also can mean the act of entering onto a computer system.

Lurking Reading Usenet newsgroups, consumer online service forums, or Internet mailing lists without posting anything, just reading. A lurker is a person who observes what everyone else is doing within that group.

Mailbot Software program that automatically responds to all incoming Email. A mailbot, or autoresponder, replies to them by sending the author a file or message.

Mailing List Manager A software program that collects and distributes e-mail messages to a mailing list.

Mail List, Mailing List A system that allows people to send e-mail to one address, whereupon their message is copied and sent to all other subscribers to the list. This method allows people with different kinds of e-mail to participate in discussions together.

Meta-Indexes A listing of Internet resources pertaining to a specific subject category, intended as a resource to those who have an interest in specific topic. A meta-index is simply a collection of URLs for related Internet resources, all arranged on a web page by their titles.

Net The shorthand version for Internet.

Netiquette Internet etiquette.

Netizen From the term "citizen," referring to a citizen of the Internet, or someone who uses networked resources.

Netpreneur An online entrepreneur.

Netscape Web browser and the name of a company. The Netscape browser was based on the Mosaic program developed at the National Center for Supercomputing Applications (NCSA).

Newbie A newcomer to the Internet

Newsgroups Name given to discussion groups on Usenet.

Password A code used to gain access to a locked system known only to one person or a specific group of individuals. Good passwords contain letters and non-letters and are not simple combinations such as *john12*.

Posting A message entered into a network communications system, such as a newsgroup submission.

Search Engine The most popular way to find resources on the Internet. There are numerous search engines each with their own unique styles and capabilities.

Server A computer, or software package, that stores information and makes these files available to other users on a network or the Internet.

Signature A block of information used at the end of every message or online document sent by that user.

Site A unique location on the Internet to post your information and get noticed.

Spam, Spamming An inappropriate attempt to use a mailing list, Usenet, or other networked communications facility as if it was a broadcast medium by sending the same message to a large number of people who didn't ask for it.

Spider An automated program that indexes documents, titles, and/or a portion of each document acquired by traversing the web.

Store Front A set location on the Web that stores and displays a collection of information about you and your business.

SQL - Structured Query Language A specialized programming language for sending queries to databases.

Telnet A program that allows people to log on to other computers or bulletin board systems on the Internet and run software remotely from their location.

Upload The transfer of a file from your computer to a server online.

URL - Uniform Resource Locator The standard way to give an address of any resource on the Internet that is part of the World Wide Web (WWW). The most common way to use a URL is to enter into a WWW browser program, such as Internet Explorer, Netscape, or Lynx and type it in the location bar.

Usenet A discussion-groups system. Comments are passed among hundreds of thousands of machines, with over 10,000 discussion areas, called newsgroups.

User session A person with a unique address that enters or re-enters a web site each day (or some other specified period). A user session is sometimes determined by counting only those users that haven't re-entered the site within the past 20 minutes or a similar period. User session figures are sometimes used to indicate the number of visitors per day.

VaporLink A link within a site on the Internet is supposed to lead to more information (hypertext). A vaporlink is one that has become nonexistent and does not lead anywhere, a dead link.

Web The shorthand version of World Wide Web.

WWW - World Wide Web The whole constellation of resources that can be accessed using Gopher, FTP, HTTP, Telnet, Usenet, WAIS, and some other tools. Also referred to as the universe of hypertext servers (HTTP servers), which are the servers that allow graphics, text, sound files, etc., to be mixed together.

Appendix B

Newsgroups

The following list of newsgroup categories is provided compliments of Lewis S. Eisen, Computer Training and Consulting, Ottawa, Ontario, Canada: *http://www.magma.ca/leisen*.

Each of these newsgroup categories has a number of sub-categories. Each sub-category will have a number of sub-sub-categories.

A

ab.	Alberta, Canada
abq.	Albuquerque, New Mexico, USA
acadia.	Acadia University, Nova Scotia, Canada
acs.	University of Calgary computer science, Alberta, Canada
adass.	Astronomical Data & Archiving Systems & Software
ahn.	Athens-Clarke County, Georgia, USA
ak.	Alaska, USA
akr.	Akron, Ohio, USA
alive.	International alternative newsgroups (obsolete)
alabama.	Alabama, USA
alc.	Newsgroups discussing alcohol
algebra.	Discussions about algebra
algonet.	Algonet, Sverige (ISP)
aol.	America Online, ISP

apana.	Australian Public Access Network Association
apc.	Association for Progressive Communications
apk.	APK Net, Ohio, USA (ISP)
ar.	Grupos de Argentina
arc.	NASA Ames Research Center, California, USA
argh.	ARGH network, Deutschland
arkane.	Arkane Systems, UK
aston.	Aston University, Birmingham, England
at.	Oesterreich (Austria)
athena.	M.I.T., Cambridge, Massachusetts, USA
atl.	Atlanta, Georgia, USA
aus.	Australian and Australasian newsgroups
austin.	Austin, Texas, USA
autodesk.	Autodesk Inc. corporate newsgroups
av.	Antelope Valley, California, USA
az.	Arizona, USA

B

ba.	San Francisco bay area, California, USA
balt.	Baltimore, Maryland, USA
baynet.	Bayerische Bürgernetze, Deutschland
burg.	Blacksburg, Virginia, USA
bc.	British Columbia, Canada
bcs.	Boston Computer Society, Massachusetts, USA
be.	Belgique/Belgïe/Belgien (Belgium)
bermuda.	Bermuda
best.	Best Internet Communications, California, USA
bhm.	Birmingham, Alabama, USA
bionet.	Biology Network
birmingham.	Birmingham, England
bison.	Manitoba, Canada
bit.	Originating from BITNET (IBM mainframe)
biz.	Usenet business newsgroups
blgtn.	Bloomington, Indiana, USA
bln.	Berlin, Germany
bnr.	Bell-Northern Research
bocaraton.	Boca Raton, Florida, USA
bochum.	Bochum, Deutschland
bologna.	Bologna, Italia
boston.	Boston, Massachusetts, USA

boulder.	Boulder, Colorado, USA
br.	Brasil
brasil.	Brasil
bremen.	Bremen, Deutschland
bremnet.	Bremen und Umgebung, Deutschland
brocku.	Brock University, Ontario, Canada
byu.	Brigham Young University, Utah, USA

C

ca.	California, USA
cabot.	Cabot College, St. John's, Newfoundland, Canada
calgary.	Calgary, Alberta, Canada
calstate.	California State University, USA
caltech.	California Institute of Technology, USA
cam.	Cambridge area, England, UK
can.	Canada
canb.	Canberra, Australia
capdist.	Albany (Capital District), New York, USA
carleton.	Carleton University, Ottawa, Ontario, Canada
cd-online.	CD-Online, Nederland (Netherlands) (ISP)
central.	Internet Company of New Zealand (ISP)
cern.	Cern, Geneva, Switzerland
ch.	Switzerland
chi.	Chicago, Illinois, USA
chile.	Chile
chinese.	China and Chinese language newsgroups
christnet.	Christian Network
cid.	Cid, Berlin, Deutschland (ISP)
cisnet.	University of Malta, Computer Info. Serv., Malta
cityscp.	Cityscape Internet Services, UK (ISP)
cityweb.	Cityweb Network GmbH, Deutschland
cl.	CL-Netz (German language newsgroups)
clari.	Clarinet News Service (commercial)
cle.	Cleveland, Ohio, USA
clinet.	Clinet, Finland (ISP)
cmc.	Chambers Multimedia Connection, Eugene, Oregon, USA (ISP)
cmh.	Columbus, Ohio, USA
cmu.	Carnegie Mellon University, USA
cna.	Chinese language newsgroups

co.	Colorado, USA
comp.	Usenet computer newsgroups
compuserve.	CompuServe (ISP)
computer42.	Computer42, Deutschland
concordia.	Concordia University, Quebec, Canada
conn.	Connecticut, USA
cor.	Corvallis, Oregon, USA
cornell.	Cornell University
courts.	United States court decisions
cov.	City of Coventry, West Midlands, UK
covuni.	Coventry University, West Midlands, UK
cs.	University of British Columbia computer science, Canada
csn.	Colorado SuperNet, USA
ct.	C't (German computer magazine)
cth.	Chalmers Univ. of Technology, Göteborg, Sverige
cu.	University of Colorado, USA
cville.	Charlottesville, Virginia and region, USA
cz.	Czech Republic newsgroups

D

dal.	Dalhousie University, Halifax, Nova Scotia, Canada
dc.	Washington, D.C., USA
ddn.	Defense Data Network, USA
dds.	Dutch Freenet language groups
de.	International German language newsgroups
delaware.	Delaware, USA
demon.	Newsgroups from the Demon network, UK
denver.	Denver, Colorado, USA
det.	Detroit, Michigan, USA
dfw.	Dallas-Ft. Worth, Texas, USA
dk.	Danmark (Denmark)
dod.	Department of Defense, USA
dortmund.	Dortmund, Deutschland
dsm.	Des Moines, Iowa, USA
dti.	Dream Train Internet Inc., Japan (ISP)
duke.	Duke University
dut.	Delft Institute of Technology, Nederland (Netherlands)

E

easynet.	Easynet, UK (ISP)

ed.	Edinburgh, Scotland
edm.	Edmonton, Alberta, Canada
ee.	Eesti (Estonia)
es.	Grupos de España
esp.	Grupos en español
eug.	Eugene/Springfield, Oregon, USA
eunet.	European Networks
example.	Bogus hierarchy reserved for standards documents
execpc.	ExecPC Internet, New Berlin, Wisconsin, USA (ISP)
eye.	Eye WEEKLY Newspaper, Toronto, Ontario, Canada

F

ffo.	Frankfurt (Oder), Deutschland
fido.	Originating from Fidonet
fido7.	Russian-language Fidonet
finet.	Finland and Finnish language alternative newsgroups
fj.	Japan and Japanese language newsgroups
fl.	Florida, USA
flora.	FLORA Community Web, Ottawa, Ontario, Canada
fnal.	Fermi National Accelerator Laboratory, Illinois, USA
fnet.	Originating from Fnet (France)
fnord.	Fnord Discordian Network
fr.	International French language newsgroups
francom.	Groupes de discussion en francais
fras.	Freie Amiga Software (German Amiga binaries)
freenet.	Groups originating from freenets
ftech.	Frontier Internet Services, UK (ISP)

G

ga.	Georgia, USA
gay-net.	German language Gay and Lesbian newsgroups
gay.	Gay and Lesbian newsgroups
gbg.	Göteborg, Sverige
geometry.	Discussions about geometry
ger.	GerNet, Deutschland (ISP)
git.	Georgia Institute of Technology, USA
gnu.	GNU operating system
gov.	Government information newsgroups
govonca.	Government of Ontario, Canada
gruene.	Partei Die Grünen/Bündnis 90, Deutschland

grk.	Greece and Greek language newsgroups
gu.	University of Göteborg, Sverige
gwu.	George Washington University, Washington, DC, USA

H

hacktic.	Dutch/English hackers' newsgroups, Nederland (Netherlands)
halcyon.	Halcyon Corporate newsgroups
hamburg.	Hamburg, Deutschland
hamilton.	Hamilton, Ontario, Canada
han.	Hangul language newsgroups (Korean)
hannet.	Hannover, Deutschland
hannover.	Hannover, Deutschland
harvard.	Harvard University, Massachusetts, USA
hawaii-online.	Hawaii-Online (ISP)
hawaii.	Hawaii, USA
hebron.	Hebron, Israel
helsinki.	Helsinki, Finland
hepnet.	High Energy Physics Network
hfx.	Halifax, Nova Scotia, Canada
hiv.	HIV-related issues
hk.	Hong Kong
hl.	Hansestadt Luebeck, Deutschland (obsolete)
hna.	Hunter Network Association, Australia (ISP)
hookup.	Hookup, Canada (ISP)
houston.	Houston, Texas, USA
hr.	Croatian newsgroups
hrnet.	Human Rights network
hsv.	Huntsville, Alabama, USA
hum.	Humber College, Etobicoke, Ontario, Canada
humanities.	Usenet discussions about humanities
hun.	Magyarorszag (Hungarian newsgroups)
hy.	University of Helsinki, Finland

I

ia.	Iowa, USA
iaf.	Internet Access Foundation, Nederland (Netherlands)
ibm.	IBM-based newsgroups
ibmnet.	IBM Global Network
ic.	ICONSULT, Deutschland (ISP)
iconz.	Internet Company of New Zealand (ISP)

idirect.	I-Direct (ISP)
ie.	Ireland
ieee.	IEEE standards (obsolete)
ihug.	The Internet Group, New Zealand (ISP)
iij.	IIJ (ISP)
iijnet.	IIJ (ISP)
il.	Illinois, USA
in.	Indiana, USA
info.	Internet technical information
inforamp.	Inforamp, Canada (ISP)
interlog.	Interlog, Canada (ISP)
israel.	Israel
it.	Italia (Italy)
ithaca.	Ithaca, New York, USA
iu.	Indiana University, Indiana, USA
iupui.	Indiana University-Purdue Univ. at Indianapolis, USA

J

japan.	Japan and Japanese language newsgroups
jaring.	Jaring network, Malaysia (ISP)
jhu.	Johns Hopkins University, Baltimore MD, USA
jogu.	Johannes-Gutenberg-Universitaet Mainz, Deutschland

K

k12.	International educational network
ka.	Karlsruhe, Deutschland
kanto.	Japanese language newsgroups
kassel.	Region Kassel, Deutschland
kc.	Kansas City, Kansas/Missouri, USA
kennesaw.	Kennesaw State University, Georgia, USA
kiel.	Kiel, Deutschland
kingston.	Kingston, Ontario, Canada
knf.	Kommunikationsnetz Franken e.V., Deutschland
knox.	Knoxville and surrounding area, Tennessee, USA
ks.	Kansas, USA
ksu.	Kansas State University, USA
kth.	Royal Institute of Technology, Stockholm, Sverige (Sweden)
kun.	Katholieke Universiteit Nijmegen, Nederlands (Netherlands)
kw.	Kitchener-Waterloo, Ontario, Canada
ky.	Kentucky, USA

L

la.	Los Angeles, California, USA
laurentian.	Laurentian University, Sudbury, Ontario, Canada
leeds.	Leeds, England
li.	Long Island, New York, USA
linux.	Linux operating system (Obsolete)
lon.	London, England
lou.	Louisiana, USA
lspace.	Discussions about Terry Pratchett
lu.	Luxembourg newsgroups
luebeck.	Luebeck, Deutschland
lv.	Latvian newsgroups

M

malta.	Malta and Maltese newsgroups
man.	Manitoba, Canada
manawatu.	Manawatu district, New Zealand
maus.	Originating from MausNet (Deutschland)
mc.	Mississippi College, Clinton, Mississippi, USA
mcgill.	McGill University, Montreal, Quebec, Canada
mcmaster.	McMaster University, Hamilton, Ontario, Canada
md.	Maryland, USA
me.	Maine, USA
medlux.	Russian language medical newsgroups
melb.	Melbourne, Australia
melbpc.	Melbourne PC User Group, Australia
memphis.	Memphis, Tennessee, USA
mensa.	Discussions among members of Mensa
metocean.	Metocean, Japan (ISP)
metropolis.	Metropolis, Nederland (ISP) (obsolete)
metu.	Middle East Technical Univ., Ankara, Turkiye
mex.	Mexican newsgroups
mi.	Michigan, USA
miami.	Miami, Florida, USA
microsoft.	Microsoft newsgroups
midlands.	English Midlands, UK
milw.	Milwaukee, Wisconsin, USA
misc.	Usenet miscellaneous newsgroups
mistral.	Brighton, England, UK
mit.	Massachusetts Institute of Technology

mn.	Minnesota, USA
mo.	Missouri, USA
ms.	Mississippi, USA
mtl.	Montreal, Quebec, Canada
mu.	Marquette University, Milwaukee, Wisconson, USA
muc.	München, Deutschland
muenster.	Muenster, Deutschland
mun.	Memorial University, Newfoundland, Canada
mv.	MV Communications, Inc. (ISP)
mx.	Mexico

N

nagasaki-u.	University of Nagasaki, Japan
nanaimo.	Nanaimo, British Columbia, Canada
nas.	NASA Numerical Aerodynamic Simulation Facility, USA
nasa.	National Aeronautics and Space Administration, USA
nashville.	Nashville, Tennessee, USA
nb.	New Brunswick, Canada
nbn.	North Bay Network, California, USA (obsolete)
nc.	North Carolina, USA
ncar.	Nat. Centre for Atmosph. Research, Colorado, USA
ncf.	National Capital Freenet, Ottawa, Ontario, Canada
ncle.	Newcastle (and Hunter Valley), Australia
ncsc.	North Carolina SuperComputing, USA
nctu.	National Chiao-Ting University, Taiwan
nd.	North Dakota, USA
ne.	New England area, USA
nebr.	Nebraska, USA
net.	Usenet II (usenet2.org)
netscape.	Netscape, Mountain View, California, USA
netz.	Originated by Netz e.V., Deutschland
nevada.	Nevada, USA
neworleans.	New Orleans, Louisiana, USA
news.	Usenet news
newsguy.	Newsguy News Service
nf.	Newfoundland, Canada
nh.	New Hampshire, USA
ni.	Northern Ireland
niagara.	Niagara Peninsula, Canada/USA
nj.	New Jersey, USA

nl.	Nederland (Netherlands)
nl-alt.	Usenet alternative nieuwsgroepen, Nederland (Netherlands)
nlnet.	Nlnet (ISP)
nm.	New Mexico, USA
no.	Norge (Norway)
nord.	Norddeutschland
nordunet.	Nordic National Research Network
north.	Weser-Ems Region, Deutschland
northwest.	Northwest region of England, UK
nrw.	Nordrhein-Westfalen, Deutschland
ns.	Nova Scotia, Canada
nu.	Newcastle University, Australia
nv.	Nevada, USA
nwt.	Northwest Territories, Canada
nwu.	Northwestern University, Illinois, USA
ny.	New York State, USA
nyc.	New York City, New York, USA
nyu.	New York University, USA
nz.	New Zealand

O

oau.	Orlando, Florida, USA
oc.	Orange County, California, USA
oerebro.	Örebro, Närke, Sverige
ogi.	Oregon Graduate Institute, USA
oh.	Ohio, USA
ok.	Oklahoma, USA
okinawa.	Okinawan newsgroups
oldenburg.	Oldenburg, Deutschland
olnet.	Oldenburg und Umgebung, Deutschland
on.	Offenes Netz Luebeck, Deutschland
online.	Telenor Online, Oslo, Norge (ISP)
ont.	Ontario, Canada
or.	Oregon, USA
osu.	Ohio State University, USA
ott.	Ottawa, Ontario, Canada
owl.	Ostwestfalen-Lippe, Deutschland
own.	One World Net
ox.	Oxford University, UK

P

pa.	Pennsylvania, USA
pb.	Der Fahrgastverband PRO BAHN, Deutschland
pdaxs.	Portland Metronet, Oregon, USA
pdx.	Portland, Oregon, USA
pei.	Prince Edward Island, Canada
peru.	Groupos del Peru
pgh.	Pittsburgh, Pennsylvania, USA
phil-priv.	The Philippines and Filipino newsgroups
phl.	Philadelphia, Pennsylvania, USA
phoenix.	Phoenix, Arizona, USA
phx.	Phoenix, Arizona, USA
pi.	Planet Internet, Nederland (Netherlands)(ISP)
pinnacle.	Pinnacle, UK (ISP)
pipex.	Pipex (ISP)
pitt.	University of Pittsburgh, Pennsylvania, USA
pl.	Polska (Polish language newsgroups)
planet.	PlaNet FreeNZ co-operative, New Zealand
pnw.	Pacific North-West (USA/Canada)
prima.	Prima e.V., Dortmund, Deutschland (ISP)
princeton.	Princeton area, New Jersey, USA
prodigy.	Prodigy (ISP)
psi.	PSINet (ISP)
psu.	Pennsylvania State University, USA
pt.	Portugal and Portuguese newsgroups
pu.	Princeton University, New Jersey, USA
pubnet.	Public Access Systems network (obsolete)
purdue.	Purdue University, Indiana, USA

Q

qc.	Quebec, Canada
queens.	Queens University, Kingston, Ontario, Canada

R

rabbit.	Rabbit Network (ISP)
rain.	RAINnet (ISP)
realtynet.	Real estate network
rec.	Usenet recreational newsgroups
redhat.	Red Hat Software, North Carolina, USA
region.	Mittlehessen, Deutschland

relcom.	Relcom, Commonwealth of Ind. States (ISP) (Cyrillic)
rg.	Rio Grande Valley, New Mexico/Texas, USA
rhein.	Rhein area (Cologne and Bonn), Germany
ri.	Rhode Island, USA
rmii.	Rocky Mountain Internet (ISP)
roanoke.	Roanoke, Virginia, USA
ru.	Rutgers University, New Jersey, USA
ruhr.	Ruhrgebiet, Deutschland
rv.	Rogue Valley, Oregon, USA
rye.	Ryerson University, Toronto, Ontario, Canada

S

saar.	Saarbruecken, Deutschland
sac.	Sacramento, California, USA
sackheads.	Sysadmins with too much time on their hands
sacramento.	Sacramento, California, USA
salford.	University of Salford, UK
sanet.	SAnet (South Africa)
sat.	San Antonio, Texas, USA
sba.	Santa Barbara, California, USA
sbay.	South Bay region, San Francisco, California, USA
schl.	Newsgroup echo of KidLink mailing-lists
schule.	German language school newsgroup
ssci.	Usenet science newsgroups
scot.	Scotland, UK
scruz.	Santa Cruz, California, USA
sd.	South Dakota, USA
sdnet.	San Diego, California, USA
se.	Sverige (Sweden)
sea.	Seattle, Washington, USA
seattle.	Seattle, Washington, USA
sfnet.	Suomi-Finland, Finland, and Finnish language newsgroups
sfu.	Simon Fraser Univ., British Columbia, Canada
sg.	Singapore
sgi.	Silicon Graphics, Inc.
shamash.	Jewish newsgroups
si.	Slovenian newsgroups
simcoe.	Simcoe County, Ontario, Canada
sj.	St. John's, Newfoundland, Canada
sk.	Saskatchewan, Canada

sk.	Slovakian newsgroups
slac.	Stanford Linear Accelerator Center, USA
slo.	San Luis Obispo, California, USA
slonet.	SLONET (ISP)
snafu.	Snafu, Deutschland (ISP)
soc.	Usenet social issues newsgroups
socs.	McGill Univ. Sch. of Comp. Sci., Quebec, Canada
sol.	Sol.net Network Services, Milwaukee, Wisconsin, USA
solent.	Solent, U.K. (ISP)
solinet.	Gewerkschaftliche Themen (German trade unions)
sonoma.	Sonoma County, California, USA
spk.	Spokane, Washington, USA
srg.	Swiss Broadcasting Corporation
srjc.	Santa Rosa Junior College, California, USA
stgt.	Stuttgart, Deutschland
stl.	St. Louis, Missouri, USA
stmarys.	St. Mary's Univ., Nova Scotia, Canada
su.	Stanford University, California
sudbury.	Sudbury, Ontario, Canada
sunet.	Swedish University Network, Sverige
surfnet.	Dutch university newsgroups, Nederland (Netherlands)
swipnet.	Swipnet Tele/2, Sverige (ISP)
swnet.	Sverige (Sweden)

T

t-netz.	German language newsgroups (obsolete)
tacoma.	Tacoma, Washington, USA
talk.	Usenet talk newsgroups
tamu.	Texas A & M University, USA
taos.	Taos, New Mexico, USA
tba.	Tampa Bay, Florida, USA
tdw.	Tidewater, Virginia, USA
tele.	Tele Danmark Internet (ISP)
terranova.	Terra Nova Visuals, Finland
thur.	Thuringia, Deutschland
tin.	TIN, Italia (Italy) (ISP)
tip.	The Internet Plaza, Nederland (Netherlands) (ISP)
tipnet.	Telia, Sverige (ISP)
tlg.	The Little Garden, California, USA (obsolete)
tn.	Tennessee, USA

tnn.	The Network News (Japanese)
tor.	Toronto, Ontario, Canada
torfree.	Toronto Freenet, Ontario, Canada
toulouse.	Toulouse, France
tp.	Toppoint, Kiel, Deutschland
tr.	Turkiye & Turkish language groups
trentu.	Trent University, Ontario, Canada
triangle.	Research Triangle Park, North Carolina, USA
trumpet.	Discussions of Trumpet programs
tulsa.	Tulsa, Oklahoma, USA
tvontario.	TVOntario, Ontario, Canada
tw.	Taiwan
tx.	Texas, USA

U

u3b.	Discussions on AT&T 3B systems
ualberta.	University of Alberta, Canada
uark.	University of Arkansas, USA
ubc.	University of British Columbia, Canada
uc.	University of California, USA
ucalgary.	University of Calgary, Alberta, Canada
ucam.	University of Cambridge, UK
ucb.	University of California at Berkeley, USA
ucd.	University of California, Davis, USA
ucsb.	Univ. of California at Santa Barbara, USA
ucsc.	University of California at Santa Cruz, USA
udes.	Universite de Sherbrooke, Quebec, Canada
uf.	University of Florida, USA
ufra.	Unterfranken, Deutschland
uiuc.	University of Illinois, Urbana-Champaign, USA
uk.	United Kingdom
ukc.	University of Kent at Canterbury, UK
ukr.	Ukraine and Ukranian language newsgroups
uky.	University of Kentucky, USA
ulaval.	Universite Laval, Quebec, Canada
um.	University of Maryland, USA
umiami.	University of Miami, Florida, USA
umich.	University of Michigan, USA
umn.	University of Minnesota, USA
umoncton.	University of Moncton, New Brunswick, Canada

umontreal.	Universite de Montreal, Quebec, Canada
unb.	University of New Brunswick, Canada
unc.	University of North Carolina at Chapel Hill, USA
unisa.	University of South Australia, Adelaide, Australia.
uo.	University of Oregon, USA
uoc.	University of Canterbury, Christchurch, New Zealand
upenn.	University of Pennsylvania, USA
uqam.	Universite du Quebec a Montreal, Canada
us.	United States
usask.	University of Saskatchewan, Canada
usf.	University of South Florida, USA
usu.	Utah State University, USA
ut.	University of Toronto, Ontario, Canada
utah.	Utah, USA
utcs.	University of Texas, Computer Science, USA
utk.	University of Tennessee, Knoxville, USA
utexas.	University of Texas, USA
uunet.	Originating from UUNet (UNIX)
uva.	University of Virgina, USA
uvic.	Univ.of Victoria, British Columbia, Canada
uw.	University of Waterloo, Ontario, Canada
uwa.	University of Washington, USA
uwarwick.	University of Warwick, UK
uwash.	University of Washington, USA
uwindsor.	University of Windsor, Ontario, Canada
uwisc.	University of Wisconsin, Madison, USA
uwm.	University of Wisconsin, Milwaukee, USA
uwo.	Univ. of Western Ontario, London, Canada

V

va.	Virginia, USA
van.	Vancouver, British Columbia, Canada
vatech.	Virginia Polytechnic Inst. and State University, USA
vechta.	Universitaet Vechta, Niedersachsen, Deutschland
vegas.	Las Vegas, Nevada, USA
vic.	Victoria, British Columbia, Canada
vmsnet.	Originating from Digital VAX network
vol.	Telecom Italia Video On Line (ISP)
vpro.	VPRO TV-station newsgroups, Nederland
vt.	Vermont, USA

vu.	Vanderbilt University

W

wa.	Western Australia
wash.	Washington, USA
westf.	Westfalen, Deutschland
wgtn.	Wellington, New Zealand (obsolete)
wi.	Wisconsin, USA
wimsey.	Wimsey, British Columia, Canada (ISP)
witten.	Witten, Deutschland
wlu.	Wilfred Laurier University, Waterloo, Ontario, Canada
wny.	Western New York, USA
worldnet.	AT&T Worldnet
worldonline.	World Online, Nederland (ISP)
wpi.	Worcester Polytechnic Institute, Massachusetts, USA
wpg.	Winnipeg, Manitoba, Canada
wv.	West Virginia, USA
wxs.	World Access/Planet Internet, Nederland (ISP)
wyo.	Wyomimg, USA

X

xs4all.	Xs4all, Nederland (ISP)

Y

yakima.	Yakima, Washington, USA
yale.	Yale University, Connecticut, USA
yk.	Yellowknife, Northwest Territories, Canada
yfn.	Youngstown, Ohio Free-Net, USA
yolo.	Yolo County, California, USA
york.	York University, Ontario, Canada
ysu.	Youngstown State University, Ohio, USA

Z

z-netz.	Originating from Z-Netz (German newsgroups)
za.	South Africa and Afrikaans newsgroups
zer.	German language newsgroups (obsolete)
zipnews.	Zippo[1]s News Services (commercial)

Appendix C

Search Engines

The Most Popular Search Engines

Alta Vista

Site Address: *http://altavista.digital.com*
Submission Address: *http://altavista.digital.com/cgi-bin/query?pg=addurl*
Alta Vista went live in December of 1995. Alta Vista is quite popular and has gained more name recognition since partnering with Yahoo! in 1996.
Pages (millions): 100 (yes that's 1 billion)
Meta Tag Support: Yes
Frames Support: No
Image Maps: Yes
Password Protected: No
# of links affects position: No
Title: Page Title, if none "No Title"
Description: Meta Tag or first text on the page

Database Refresh: Monthly or longer
Time to index submissions: 1 day
Type: Spider

AOL NetFind

Site Address: *www.aol.com/netfind/*
Submission Address: *www.aol.com/netfind/info/addyoursite.html*
AOL NetFind is a copy of Excite. They use the same technology with different names. All of the capabilities and tips associated with Excite are the same for AOL NetFind.

Excite

Site Address: *http://www.excite.com*
Submission Address: click on "Suggest site" at www.excite.com
Has been around since 1995. Excite bought out WebCrawler and Magellan in 1996. These acquisitions are still independently operated.
Pages (millions): 55
Meta Tag Support: No
Frames Support: No
Image Maps: No
Password Protected: Yes
# of links affects position: No
Title: Page Title, if none "Untitled"
Description: The few most dominant sentences on your pages.
Database Refresh: Weekly
Time to index submissions: 3 weeks
Type: Directory
Tips: Make the first few 100 characters on your page as descriptive as possible. Excite will try to make the description from the text at the start of your page but will keep going until it is satisfied that it has enough descriptive sentences. Your sentences must be complete for Excite to use them in forming your description. This does not necessarily mean that uncompleted sentences at the beginning of your page will not be used. Excite would just rather use complete sentences.

HotBot

Site Address: *http://www.hotbot.com*
Submission Address: *http://www.hotbot.com/addurl.asp*

HotBot was launched in 1996 and is owned by *Wired*. HotBot uses the same search engine technology as Inktomi.
Pages (millions): over 54
Meta Tag Support: Yes
Frames Support: No
Image Maps: No
Password Protected: No
# of links affects position: Yes
Title: Page Title, if none URL
Description: Meta Tag, if none first few sentences in body
Database Refresh: Monthly or longer.
Average Submission Time: 4 weeks
Tips: If you do a search and feel that your site was not positioned correctly in the search results, then you can let the people at HotBot know about it. Send all the relevant information to *bugs@hotbot.com.*

InfoSeek

Site Address: *http://www.infoseek.com*
Submission Address: *www-request@infoseek.com*
InfoSeek has been online since 1995. It is a very well-known search engine. InfoSeek also manages a directory separate from its search engine. Sites are listed categorically and some are even reviewed and recommended by InfoSeek.
Pages (millions): 50
Meta Tag Support: Yes
FramesSupport: Yes
Image Maps: Yes
Alt attribute: Yes
Password Protected: Yes
# of links affects position: No
Title: Page Title, if none first line on the page
Description: The Meta Tag, if none the first 200 characters in the body
Database Refresh: 3 weeks
Time to index submissions: minutes
Tips: Use the alt attribute because InfoSeek will include these in your description. You will have better chances that they get it right. This is especially helpful for sites that are mainly graphical in content.

Lycos

Site Address: *http://www.lycos.com*
Submission Address: *http:// www.lycos.com/register.html*
Lycos went online in 1994. Lycos is a well-recognized spider.
Pages (millions): 30
Meta Tag Support: Yes
Frames Support: Yes
Image Maps: No
Password Protected: Yes
# of links affects position: Yes
Title: Page Title, if none the first line of the page
Description: A snippet of the page that has been determined to represent it.
Database Refresh: 2 weeks
Time to index submissions: 3 weeks
Type: Spider
Tips: Don't have an image map at the beginning of your page because Lycos won't be able to read it.

WebCrawler

Site Address: *http://www.webcrawler.com*
Submission Address: *http://www.webcrawler.com/WebCrawler/SubmitURLS.html*
WebCrawler has been around since 1994 and has since been purchased twice. It is now owned by Excite, but is still operated independently.
Pages (millions): 2
Meta Tag Support: Yes
Frames Support: No
Image Maps: Yes
Password Protected: No
# of links affects position: Yes
Title: Page Title, if none URL
Description: Meta Tag, if none the first 275 characters in the body
Database Refresh: Weekly
Average Submission Time: 4 weeks
Type: Spider/Crawler
Tips: Your position in WebCrawler is affected by the number of links you have to your site. If other sites have more links to them they may be ranked more highly in search results.

Yahoo!

Site Address: *http://www.yahoo.com*
Submission Address: *http://add.yahoo.com/bin/add?*
Established in 1994, Yahoo! is a well-recognized directory. It is the largest of its kind and is popular with Internet users. Yahoo! is a directory, but it does not read pages on the net like the other search engines discussed here. To have your site added to Yahoo!, you must fill out a submit form on the site. You must register your site in a category and your site is checked by employees to verify that it matches the category you have chosen. If your site is commercial in any way, you must register it in a sub-category of Business and Economy.
Pages: 500,000+
Tips: Yahoo! uses keywords found in the "Title" and "Comments" field to index your site. When filling out the form, look at these fields especially and see if there is are sufficient keywords to index your site. If anything important is missing, work it into one of these fields.

Other Search Engines and Directories

555-1212.com

Site Address: *http://www.555-1212.com*
Submission Address: *http:// www.555-1212.com/addbiz.html*
In addition to Area Code Lookup, you can shop online, find businesses near you, get your friends' telephone numbers and e-mail addresses, browse classified ads, and much more.

AAA1biz

Site Address: *http://www.aaa1biz.com/database/search.html*
Submission Address: *http://www.aaa1biz.com/database/post.html*

The Biz

Site Address: *http://www.thebiz.co.uk*
Submission Address: *http://www.thebiz.co.uk/submit.htm*
The Business Information Zone has been developed for users seeking UK-relevant business information, products, and services on the Internet, whether users are in the UK or overseas.

BizWeb

Site Address: *http://www.bizweb.com*
Submission Address: *submission@bizweb.com*
BizWeb is a web business guide to 43,165 companies listed in 194 categories.

Business Seek

Site Address: *http://www.businesseek.com*
Submission Address: *http://www.businesseek.com/business/engalta.htm*
This is the first exclusive search of business. You can add your company in different languages. There are more than 150,000 using this service.

Canadian Internet Business Directory, The

Site Address: *http://www.cibd.com/Districts.htm*
Submission Address: *http://cibd.com/cibd/add.html*

GoTo.com

Site Address: *http://www.goto.com*
Submission Address: *http://www.goto.com/d/about/howto/ht_linkto.jhtml*
GoTo is the one of the fastest, easiest, most relevant search engine on the web, as well as the small advertiser's best friend.

Infomak.com

Site Address: *http://www.infomak.com*
Submission Address: *http://www.infomak.com/add_url.sh*
Free web site promotion, free classifieds, daily horoscope, weather, local and international news chat, and more.

Internet Promotions MegaList

Site Address: *http://www.2020tech.com*
Submission Address: *http://www.2020tech.com/submit.html*
20/20 Technologies is a one-stop Internet advertising solution. Their services include web page design, Internet research, and Internet promotions.

Linkaholics

Site Address: *http://shanghai.gs180.net/linkaholics*
Submission Address: *http://shanghai.gs180.net/linkaholics/addlink.asp*
This is a self-perpetuating list of links to start your web journey. Add your link to the list and as new links are added old ones fall off. There is always a fresh batch of links.

Linkcentre Directory

Site Address: *http://linkcentre.com*
Submission Address: *http://linkcentre.com/addurl.html*
Search the Linkcentre Directory or add your web page immediately for greater exposure on the Internet.

LinkStar Internet Directory

Site Address: *http://www.linkstar.com*
Submission Address: *http:/www.linkstar.com/linkstar/bin/do form?form=ecard*
The LinkStar Business Directory is one of the Internet's most accurate business-oriented search engines, containing more than 320,000 user-entered listings. Internet users can easily find real contact information on what they're looking for, including e-mail and web addresses, more accurately than just about anywhere else online.

Manufacturers Information Net

Site Address: *http://mfginfo.com*
Submission Address: *http://mfginfo.com/htm/infoform.htm*
This site provides a complete source of information for industry and those services related to manufacturing. Use the search engine to locate information on manufacturers, suppliers, professional services, and many more resources on and off this web site.

McKinley's Internet Directory

Site Address: *http://www.mckinley.com*
Submission Address: *http://www.mckinley.com/magellan/Info/addsite.html*
Magellan's technology offers a unique way to search the web: by concept. Like most search engines, they've programmed this search engine to look for documents containing the exact words you entered into the query box. But magellan goes further and looks for ideas closely linked to the words in your query. This feature broadens your search.

Nerd World

Site Address: *http://www.nerdworld.com*
Submission Address: *http://www.nerdworld.com/nwadd.html*
Nerd World's most prominent feature is their search engine and subject index.

Small Business

Site Address: *http://www.bizoffice.com*
Submission Address: *http://www.bizoffice.com/submit.html*
Small and home-based business links. Hundreds of links to quality sites.

Trade Wave Galaxy

Site Address: *http://www.einet.net/galaxy.html*
Submission Address: *http://www.einet.net/cgi-bin/annotate?/galaxy*
Galaxy is known as the professional's guide to a world of information.

What-U-Seek

Site Address: *http://whatuseek.com*
Submission Address: *http://www.whatuseek.com/addurl.html*

Search Engine Lists and Information

If you want to find a current list of all the search engines available for submission of your site, or if you need more information on search engines, bots, and other intelligent agents, check these sites:

Search Engine Watch

http://www.searchenginewatch.com
Be sure to sign up for the Search Engine Report Mailing List.

The Big Search Engine Index

http://www.merrydew.demon.co.uk/search.htm
This site provides a list of hundreds of search engines divided into categories.

Appendix D

Internet Marketing Resources

Internet Resources for each topic covered in the book are located at the end of each chapter. Here, additionally, we have included a number of great Internet marketing resource sites.

A1 WWW Promotion Sites
http://www.a1co.com
Excellent resource for locating hundreds of directories, indexes, and catalogs that will list your site for free. Also has a handy tool for locating large e-zine sites.

Al Czarnecki Communications
http://www.web.net/alcom
A communications site with tips and resources to help you build important relationships, public relations, social marketing, and fund raising.

Connex Network Incorporated
http://www.connexnetwork.com
Connex Network provides consulting services to companies interested in marketing on the Internet. Their Web Site Report Card reviews your site against 50 criteria and provides feedback to assist you in improving your site from a marketing perspective. Their Internet marketing strategies are pre-

pared specifically for your company with your objectives, your products and services, and your target customers in mind. Connex also delivers general and company-specific Internet Marketing Workshops. Connex Network Incorporated is owned by the author of this book.

CyberPulse
http://www.cyberpulse.com
Bob and Varda Novick know their stuff when it comes to online marketing. Excellent resource area covering mailing lists, newsgroups, advertising, promotion, etc. Don't let the plain graphics fool you.

Deadlock Dispatch
http://www.deadlock.com/promote
If you're really serious about your promotion campaign, there's a whole new world of in-depth articles and really clever online marketing strategies one mouse-click away.

Directory of Ezines
http://www.lifestylespub.com/cgi-bin/ezines.cgi?10166
Lifestyles is the presenter of The Directory of Ezines, a well-researched, up-to-date list of internet newsletters that accept classified advertising. Each listing within The Directory of Ezines tells you everything you need to know about advertising in a specific newsletter.

Dominis Interactive Ezines
http://www.dominis.com/Zines
This site lists about 3,000 ezine publications. They also feature lists of the 100 popular ezines and the 100 hot ezines. If you plan to publish an e-mail newsletter, be sure to get it listed here.

Executive Summary
http://www.x-summary.com
A content-rich site and newsletter dedicated to Internet marketing trends, profiles, news, and advice.

E Weekly
http://www.eweekly.com
An online newsletter that contains articles on small business and Internet commerce and marketing. Back issues are also available. There are a number of connections to projects of the sponsor, Cyber Media.

Gator's Bite
http://www.gators-byte.com
A weekly column dedicated to helping your potential customers find your site, and keep coming back! You can join the Gator's mailing list that sends you the weekly information. Check out past articles as well.

InfoScavenger
http://www.infoscavenger.com/engine.htm
This site provides an annotated hotlist of resources to help you get your web page to appear at the top of the list when someone uses AltaVista, InfoSeek, or other engines to find you. This web site has a nice, specific mission.

Internet Marketing Issues
http://www.intersuccess.com/imi
A free weekly publication providing help to thousands of home-based and small business owners around the globe. Every issue of IMI features **online** marketing tips, techniques, and secrets aimed at helping you explode your online profits.

Marketing SuperSite
http://www.ntu.edu.sg/library/advrtise.htm
This resource list from the National Technology University in Singapore is almost too big. Contains links to a massive number of articles and web sites concerned with promotion, marketing, and commerce on the Internet.

Meta Tag Builder
http://www.MetaTagBuilder.com
This free area (provided by NetPromote) helps site owners create Meta Tags in the correct format simply by inputting web site information and clicking a button.

NetPromote
http://www.NetPromote.com
This site provides a free web promotion service for companies and individuals. NetPromote also offers consulting services that guarantee top-20 placement on the major search engines, plus unlimited resubmissions to the best search engines for life, for free.

Promotion 101
http://www.Promotion101.com
This division of NetPromote provides a free online tutorial to help web site owners learn how to better their placement on search engines and increase traffic to their sites. Includes the Ultimate Top 20 Search Engine Placement Guide. Also articles on optimizing web pages.

Public Relations Online Resources
http://www.impulse-research.com/impulse/resource.html
An excellent set of links from Impulse Research Corporation covering PR services, associations, self-promotion sites, people finders, and various online publications. Links are annotated and kept up to date.

SelfPromotion.com
http://selfpromotion.com
Automatically add your URL for free to over 100 of the biggest and most important indexes and search engines! Apply for hundreds of awards and improve your ranking in the search engines.

Submit It!
http://www.submit-it.com
Free service to register your site with the top 20 (plus or minus) directories and catalogs. A real time-saver!

VeryHot.com
http://www.veryhot.com
Links to many great Internet marketing tools.

Virtual Promote: Promote or Die!
http://www.virtualpromote.com/home.html
A great source of information and tools to get your site noticed.

Web Resources
http://www.webresource.net
Lots of good information on HTML and creating and maintaining a web site.

Website Promotion Tools
http://www.newapps.com/appstopics/Win_95_Web_Site_Promotion_Tools.html
A large list of programs of interest to web masters to help in web site promotion.

WebStep 100
http://www.mmgco.com/top100.html
John Audette of Multimedia Marketing Group put together this list of the top 100 directories, indexes, and catalogs. The links are all annotated, and you can get to each site's registration page from the link on WebStep.

Webmaster Resources
http://www.webmaster-resources.com
A handy and useful site for helping you design your own web site. Good advice, lots of links, and plenty of useful information about web hosting companies, awards, tracking programs, mailing list servers, web site promotion, and sponsorships.

The WebMaster's Notebook
http://www.cio.com/WebMaster/wm_notebook_front.html
This comprehensive site contains information of value to anyone that runs, or wants to, a WWW site: tools and links, technology notes, online web seminars, web reports, and the WebMaster Magazine.

Webmasters' Guild
http://www.webmaster.org/
Non-profit, professional organization for web masters—to disseminate information and discuss issues of concerns to web masters: network configuration, interface and graphical design, software development, business strategy, writing, marketing, and project management.

Webmaster Magazine
http://www.web-master.com
An electronic magazine that examines the use of the web by, and within, business. Topics include how companies are using the web to improve operations, reduce expenses, and connect to their customers.

Webmaster Reference Library
http://webreference.com
More than 700 carefully selected and annotated web sites and articles of interest to web masters. Site includes web wizard of the month, what's new, and feedback area.

WebPromote Weekly
http://www.WebPromote.com/wpweekly
A leading web site marketing newsletter. Very useful for your marketing strategy.

WebWorkers TOP 10 Web Business Directories
http://www.webworker.com
Resources for creating and promoting an **online** business. Outstanding web business opportunities and web business services that enable the prospective entrepreneur to be successful.

The Weekly Bookmark Distribution List
http://www.webcom.com/weekly
A distribution list, "webletter" announces new sites on the World Wide Web. Each issue contains links to news articles from various sources on the web and 10 to 20 new or updated sites from around the Internet.

Who's Marketing Online
http://www.wmo.com
A weekly online magazine that provides articles and resources about marketing online. This site provides past articles, daily and weekly updates, and a powerful link library that accesses several large directories of web information from a central page. Useful for advertising and styles to help you design an effective web site.

Wilson Internet Services
http://www.wilsonweb.com/webmarket
This site links to marketing information (more than 225 online articles primarily directed towards marketing small businesses on the web). Topics include how to design a web site, how to market on the web, and marketing theory.

Appendix E

Implementation and Maintenance Schedule

To accomplish the best results from your Internet marketing strategy, you should develop an Implementation and Maintenance Schedule.

Schedule

Every Implementation and Maintenance Schedule will be different since every company's Internet marketing strategy will be different. See Figure E-1 for a sample schedule. We have provided brief explanations in the following paragraphs to help further clarify the items included in this sample.

Search Engine Submissions

You should take your list of directory and search engine submissions and divide it into four groups. Weekly, you should take one group, go to

Name	Weekly	Bi-Weekly	Monthly	Bi-Monthly	Quarterly	Yearly
Search Engine Submissions	✓					
Press Release				✓		
Banner			✓			
Advertising						
Update/ Rename Titles			✓			
Cool Sites			✓			
Check Competitors				✓		
Cybermalls					✓	
Newsletter			✓			
Newsgroups	✓					
Mailing Lists			✓			
Guest Book	✓					
Sig Files			✓			
Links		✓				
What's New	✓					
Calendar of Events	✓					
Employment Opportunities	✓					
Offline Promotion					✓	
Tune-up					✓	
Web Browser Testing			✓			

Figure E.1. Implementation and Maintenance Schedule.

each of the directories and search engines in that group and search for your company by name and also by several key words. If you appear in the first 10 to 20 search rankings and are happy with the description, you don't have to do anything with that search engine or directory.

If, however, you do not appear or are not satisfied with the description, you should resubmit all your pages to that directory or search engine. The search engines and directories purge their databases from time to time to ensure all entries are current. The next week take the next group and go through the same process. This way you check every directory and search engine at least monthly to ensure you are still there and easily accessible.

Press Releases

Press releases should be scheduled at least bi-monthly. If you have a major announcement the press releases may be more frequent.

Banner Advertising

Check banner advertising locations of your ads. Determine the effectiveness of these ads and look for new sites for more exposure. Check prices and traffic flow of these new sites to determine how relevant they may be in increasing the traffic to your site. Adjust your banner advertising strategy accordingly.

Title Pages

Update and retitle your pages monthly unless you add a new section that requires more frequent updates (for example, Tip of the Week). Retitling your pages and updating your site is useful for two main reasons. First, spiders, crawlers, and bots are continuously visiting sites to see if there have been changes (they update their information accordingly). Second, many of your site visitors use software that lets them know when their bookmarked sites have been updated. They will only revisit your site when they know there have been changes.

Cool Sites

Submit to Cool Sites, Site of the Day, or Top 5%. In order to better your chances of becoming one, you should check on how often to apply, usually monthly.

Check of Competitors

You should regularly review your competitors' sites.

Cybermalls

Cybermalls continually change, as does everything, so do a quick check to find new malls or changes to the ones that interest you.

Newsletter

A newsletter should be scheduled monthly so you are getting your name and information in front of clients and potential clients on a regular basis.

Newsgroups

Newsgroups that you participate in should be visited every couple of days and you should try to post messages. The more often you post, particularly providing answers to queries or assistance, the more recognized and valued you are (and is your expertise). Make sure you have the sig file attached for maximum marketing effect.

Mailing Lists

There are new mail lists appearing daily. Review (and update if appropriate) those that you participate in on a monthly basis.

Guest Book

Your guest book should be checked and monitored so you can see who is visiting and what they have to say. Weekly you should copy the new contact list to the appropriate databases (e-mail lists, newsletter, etc.).

Sig Files

Keep your sig files current. Review and change them on a regular basis with new information or achievements.

Links

The more reciprocal links you can get the better. You should constantly be looking for additional, appropriate sites from which to be linked. As a minimum, you should schedule time bi-weekly to actively seek appropriate link sites.

What's New

Your What's New Page should be updated regularly, weekly if possible.

Calendar of Events

If you choose to have a calendar of events on your site, ensure that it is kept current, at least updated weekly.

Employment Opportunities

This section should also be monitored and updated weekly, deleting positions that have been filled and adding new positions as they become available.

Offline Promotion

Make sure that your offline marketing materials and your online materials are consistent (message, logos, corporate colors, etc.). Also ensure that, where appropriate, you include your URL in your offline promotion materials. This should be checked at least quarterly.

Tune-Ups

Tune-ups should be done quarterly unless changes are made to the site. One location to check is Web Site Garage at *http://www.websitegarage.com*. Here you can check spelling, browser compatibility, HTML design, link popularity, load time, and much more.

WebBrowser Testing

Test your site with the major web browsers. This should be done whenever there is a new release of Netscape or Internet Explorer. You should check monthly to determine if there have been new releases.

Index

Reader Feedback Sheet

Your comments and suggestions are very important in shaping future publications. Please e-mail us at *moreinfo@maxpress.com* (please cc: the author at *susan@connexnetwork.com)* or photocopy this page, jot down your thoughts, and fax it to (850) 934-9981 or mail it to:

Maximum Press

Attn: Jim Hoskins

605 Silverthorn Road

Gulf Breeze, FL 32561

Marketing on the Internet, Third Edition
by Jan Zimmerman and Michael Mathiesen
445 pages, illustrations
$34.95
ISBN: 1-885068-26-3

Exploring IBM's Bold Internet Strategy
by Jim Hoskins and Vince Lupiano
184 pages
$34.95
ISBN: 1-885068-23-9

Exploring IBM Technology and Products
edited by Jim Hoskins
232 pages, paper
$54.95
ISBN: 1-885068-29-8

Exploring IBM's New Age Mainframes, Fifth Edition
by Jim Hoskins and Jim Fletcher
448 pages, illustrations
$39.95
ISBN: 1-885068-15-8

Building Intranets with Lotus Notes & Domino, Second Edition
by Steve Krantz
$32.95
ISBN: 1-885068-24-7

Exploring IBM Client/Server Computing
by David Bolthouse
471 pages, illustrations
$32.95
ISBN: 1-885068-04-2

Exploring IBM RS/6000 Computers, Eighth Edition
by Jim Hoskins and Doug Davies
423 pages, illustrations
$39.95
ISBN: 1-885068-20-4

Exploring IBM AS/400 Computers, Eighth Edition
by Jim Hoskins and Roger Dimmick
502 pages, illustrations
$39.95
ISBN: 1-885068-19-0

To purchase a Maximum Press book, visit your local bookstore or call 1-800-989-6733 (US) or 1-850-934-4583 (International) or visit our homepage: ***www.maxpress.com***

Exploring the PowerPC Revolution! Second Edition
by Jim Hoskins and Jack Blackledge
165 pages, illustrations
$22.95
ISBN: 1-885068-02-6

Business-to-Business Internet Marketing
by Barry Silverstein
425 pages, illustrations
$19.95
ISBN: 1-885068-35-2

Dr. Livingstone's On-line Shopping Safari Guidebook
by Frank Fiore
501 pages, illustrations
$24.95
ISBN: 1-885068-07-7

Exploring IBM Personal Computers, Ninth Edition
by Jim Hoskins and Bill Wilson,
360 pages, illustrations
$34.95
ISBN: 1-885068-12-3

Real World Client/Server
by Steve Krantz
344 pages, illustrations
$29.95
ISBN: 0-9633214-7-1

Exploring the IBM AS/400 Advanced 36, Second Edition
by Jim Hoskins and Roger Dimmick
105 pages, illustrations
$26.95
ISBN: 1-885068-11-5

What About ProductManager?
by David Curtis
200 pages, illustrations
$34.95
ISBN: 0-9633214-4-7

Exploring IBM Print on Demand Technology
by Jim Wallace
122 pages, illustrations
$22.95
ISBN: 1-885068-06-9

To purchase a Maximum Press book, visit your local bookstore or call 1-800-989-6733 (US/Canada) or 1-850-934-4583 (International) or visit our homepage: ***www.maxpress.com***